CW00839813

The Things I Wish I Knew Before Becoming a Teacher

The HONEST handbook for trainees, newly qualified teachers and recently qualified teachers.

The Things I Wish I Knew Before Becoming a Teacher

Tim Mobbs

Written by Tim Mobbs

Cover Design by Flat Cap Design Ltd
(www.thinkflatcap.com)

Copyright © Tim Mobbs 2018

Thank you to my wonderful wife
Aimee for her unwavering love,
designs and support and my
beautiful daughter Millie for making
the world one big adventure.

Contents:

P.7   Preface

P.8   Introduction

P.11   Settling in to school

P.22   Wellbeing

P.33   Home Life

P.39   Wider School Life

P.48   Behaviour Management

P.55   Classroom Teaching

P.91   Personal Development

P.113   Relationships

P.123   Teaching Practice

P.141   The World of Education

P.147   Thank You

Preface

I have written this book to help those of you who are just starting, or are still early in your career. If you are looking for a book full of teaching theory then this is not it. If you are hoping for evidential support for my opinions you will not find it here. These are the things I have discovered by living and breathing the life of a teacher, day in and day out for years. My aim for this book is to help you learn from my mistakes so you don't make them yourself and to be aware of some common frustrations so they do not take you by surprise (like they did to me). I have included many, practical ideas to save time, manage your classroom, manage behaviour, be an effective member of school and look after yourself.

If I could meet my former self for a coffee and have a chat then I would put my arm around my younger shoulders and tell myself the following...

Introduction:

I came into teaching by accident after I made the decision to leave a highly-ranked graduate scheme, and didn't really have a plan. I approached my old secondary school and asked if I could coach a rugby team whilst I searched for a new job. Somehow, I became a Teaching Assistant working with GCSE students on the C/D borderline for maths. I fell in love with the challenging, wonderful, maddening, frustrating, side-splittingly-funny, emotional world of education.

After 18 months I was accepted to the TeachFirst leadership development programme – I applied to be a history teacher but was guided towards primary education (a move I am very glad I made). I have taught many fantastic children; mentored great students/trainees, newly qualified teachers, and recently qualified teachers; led key stage 2; and led maths, writing and reading in several schools. Writing this book has made me think back to the challenging, early days of becoming a teacher and pin point situations that I wish I had been aware of before I stumbled into them tired and bleary eyed.

When I arrived in school on my first day as a student teacher, I was nervous and excited. I immediately started noticing many things about the inner workings of school and the wider environment of education. For example, how easy it is to make a basic mistake due to the huge amount of plates you will spin:

I entered my first classroom that I was sharing with my mentor. It was all set up for the new year with displays, resources, books and routines in their correct place. As I wandered round, I noticed the topic display with the proud title: Australia. I continued my walk round but something wasn't right. I returned to the Australia display and realised that the lettering was filled with hundreds of American flags, rather than Australian. Lesson – mistakes can be made very easily when you are trying to do a hundred things at once.

What follows are the things I have realised through my own experience that would have helped me, and will hopefully help you, through my early days in the classroom. I have grouped them into areas of teaching life but they are in no order of importance. I hope that if you are a student or NQT you gain some value from these chapters and if you are an experienced teacher you identify and find humour in my observations.

If you want more or to discuss anything you read please follow me on:

Twitter: @sirmobbsalot

Facebook:
https://www.facebook.com/sirmobbsalot/

Blog:
https://bebetterteachingblog.wordpress.com/
where you can join my mailing list to hear regular hints and tips and about my new publications.

The things I wish I knew about...

Settling In To School

Make sure you go to the staffroom regularly.

Teaching is a busy, full on job. You could and probably will work through lunchtimes and well beyond the end of the day. I certainly did. I also realised that there were days that I didn't spend time with anyone other than my class and the odd conversation with my teaching assistant. This is not healthy. Try to get to know the team you are part of and spend time in the staffroom or you will feel very isolated very quickly.

No school is the same as another school.

I was surprised at the lack of consistency within education. I assumed that systems and policies would be in place and working as the school system is so well established. In my experience, there are regular policy and emphasis changes (normally politically motivated), which means schools are constantly evolving and adjusting. This leads to a situation where one head teacher may want something done one way whereas another head teacher may want it done in a completely different way. A common example is the sheer amount of and wide-ranging behaviour policies and systems used in schools.

Early in your career, learn your school culture and stick to it. You are more than entitled to question things if you truly disagree but I suggest you concentrate on learning the art of teaching before worrying about wider policies. I used a lot of energy trying to make an impact across the wider school when I should have perhaps spent it on my personal development as a teacher.

There is no one way to do things within the education system.

There are many schools of thought on how teaching and learning should occur. You will not be a successful teacher unless you are yourself and stick to what you believe. I suggest you analyse yourself and decide what kind of teacher you want to be. As you teach more and more you will try things that work really well and other things that don't work at all. Every day in the classroom will shape your thinking about education. As long as the children are safe, happy and learning then how that happens is not necessary. Personally, I believe in active, fun and relevant learning where a lot of the time I am a facilitator.

Always present a positive outlook to children and other staff.

Radiator or Drain? You will come across both types of people in all walks of life but there is no place like a staffroom to be a microcosm of society. Drains are very dangerous as morale of a school staff is such a delicate thing. You will always get drains who moan at every opportunity –

"Behaviour is so bad."

"No one understands how hard it is."

"Leaders never support us."

"My class is the worst."

…the feedback they had from their observation was unfair, it's raining but they have to go on duty and so on and so on. It's draining just writing this and I'm sure for you reading it!

I challenge you to make the conscious decision to be a radiator. Be positive. Smile. Don't get sucked into the moaning. The immediate impact you can have on a school is raising morale for all (adults and children), by smiling. Things can be tough in schools but there are lots of amazing things happening as well. Find these and shout about them. Tell someone their display is amazing. Catch children being good. Thank someone for their help or support. Make someone a cup of tea or coffee. Constant positive messaging to all you come in contact too will have an enormous impact on the wider morale within school. Do not succumb to the negative arm that some will try and metaphorically or literally wrap around your shoulder and try and lead you to the 'dark side'.

When you do have to vent about something (and you will have to), choose an appropriate time, place and person. The staffroom is not it!

Senior management are humans – talk to them.

Senior leaders are not psychic but in my experience adults in schools seem to think they are. I have been guilty of this. Communication is extremely important and can be one of the first things that stops working when you are in the middle of a busy term. If something is going wrong, breaks or happens then let the relevant people know as soon as possible. E-mail is great but nothing works like a quick face to face conversation. They will appreciate you taking the time to talk to them.

Do the expected things well.

Every school have things they focus on more than any other. Work out quickly what these are at your school and make sure you do them well. It might be that there is a focus on reading corners – make yours the best. It might be 'working walls'- make sure yours is updated regularly. It might be a particular feedback system – stay on top of it. When leaders launch an initiative, it is their job to ensure this happens – they are under pressure from their leaders and will have a great focus on that particular thing until they can show it is successful. Play the 'game' and make sure you are ticking the boxes that are going to be looked at.

Get to know all support staff and their names.

I am ashamed to admit that when I left my first school, after three years, there were still members of staff who I did not know by name. I was so busy learning to teach that I didn't make the effort to get to know people. Then it got to the point where it was too late to ask them. It is important that you get to know the wider team, as you never know when you might need a favour. Also, its polite.

Action any new initiatives straight away and make it obvious.

This is similar to the point I made previously about ticking the boxes you have to. If a new initiative is introduced then it is definitely going to be checked soon after. There is nothing worse than being the person who hadn't quite got around to it when monitoring took place. It doesn't matter how busy you are, make sure you do it as soon as possible. Delegate if you must but get it done!

If you borrow something, give it back.

This is common sense but, again, it is easy to borrow something and forget. Other adults are also busy and it is very frustrating if, for example, you need to staple something and the person down the hall borrowed your stapler and didn't bring it back because then you must waste your own time going to find it. Time is precious – don't waste your own or other's. You will soon get a reputation and will then find that people seem to never have the thing you are asking to borrow.

If you use something, put it away.

Whenever you make a mess or use equipment, especially in communal areas, make sure you put it away straight away. You might be intending to do it the following morning but someone may think you have forgotten and do it for you. This can lead to resentment and a reputation for being messy. I suggest that before you move onto a new task, get the last one tidied away (get your class to help – kids love jobs).

Mini-whiteboards are amazing... they destroy books.

Mini-whiteboards are a great resource for a range of activities but no matter how careful you ask your children to be, as soon as a work book goes near a mini-whiteboard it will become covered in black gunge and you will not be able to rescue it. If you want to avoid this then don't have books and whiteboards out at the same time, or back your books.

Keep reserves of stationery... Children consume resources.

Even if you do this, you will probably still run out by the summer term. Schools can become black markets where those who have carefully hoarded equipment become the king pins and all others are beholden to them. On a serious note, keep a supply of resources like glue sticks, pens, pencils, post it notes, blu-tac and Sellotape and divide it into 3 boxes (one for each term). I have tried many things: labelling pens and pencils with names, pencil cases, handing out and collecting in each lesson and many more strategies. No matter what I have tried I have never solved the equipment crisis of summer term.

Is laminating worth the time and cost?

Laminating takes a large amount of time and is a relatively expensive activity; I have found it is rarely worth it (to the point I don't do it at all now). If you laminate work for a display, it will keep well but no one will be able to read it because it will be too shiny. If you laminate a resource for a lesson and use it once, then you have wasted a lot of precious time and money. On the other hand, if you laminate a resource and use it regularly then it is well worth it.

I once observed an excellent student teacher who had created red and yellow cards for every child to use for an activity in his lesson. Each card was laminated. 30 children, 2 cards each = 60 cards and a huge amount of time and money spent laminating. The children used the cards for no more than 45 seconds. When I asked the student how long it had taken to laminate the cards he replied, "Over 2 hours." When I asked if he intended to use them again he replied, "Probably not." This is an example of preparation time far exceeding the benefit in the lesson. The choice is yours but before firing up the laminator ask yourself – is it worth it?

Keep ICT resources organised.

I have many memory sticks and folders on my computer full of resources. I probably have at least 6 different folders called "English Resources". I have been terrible at keeping my computer based resources organised. There have been many occasions when I have wanted to re-use something and have spent longer trawling through my computers than it would have taken to remake it. Organisation on ICT is as important as organisation of paperwork, timetables, diary etc. Be organised, save time.

You will question why you became a teacher.

At various points during your career you will question why you became a teacher. I do regularly – normally towards the end of terms (because I'm shattered) and the start of each year (because new classes are challenging). It's so important to remember all the amazing things that happen every day.

When my first class left for secondary school (after I had them for two years) my wife secretly asked my teaching assistant to get them all to draw a self-portrait and write me a message. I still look at this all these years later and it reminds me of the reason I became a teacher – to make a real and lasting difference in children's lives.

Keep marking pens safe – they quickly disappear.

Marking pens disappear. They just do. They also explode in your pocket regularly or turn up under car seats or in back packs. My best teacher purchase was a fountain pen. I kept it on my lanyard, the children love it and I am yet to lose it.

The things I wish I knew about...

Wellbeing

You will always have more work you could do.

You must give yourself permission to say enough is enough. You could work every second you are awake and still have work to do. You will dream about work – some of my greatest lessons have been based on school dreams! It is important to set yourself limits and know when to stop. Prioritise and 'don't sweat the small stuff'.

Teaching feels like you are on a treadmill – that's why you are so tired all the time.

There is no end to your 'to do list'. Your job is never complete because there is always something else to do. You go on and on and on planning, delivering, marking, reflecting, planning, delivering, marking reflecting and so on and on. You need to rest and sleep when you can. Although many in teaching seem to have the self-harm mindset of work until you drop, that is not the way. If you are too tired then you can't be your best self and it is your best self that your pupils need and deserve. It is absolutely fine not to reach the end of your to do list... there is always tomorrow.

Don't be scared/too proud to ask for help.

As a student teacher I went through periods where I really struggled. I could not seem to make sense of things that seemed to be easy to other teachers. I told a colleague that I was struggling and got the response of, "That's teaching." Well, that isn't teaching at all! Would we tell a struggling pupil that "That's school."? No, we wouldn't. My colleague failed me here by not giving or guiding me towards support.

You will find things hard. You must ask for help whether from a mentor, a tutor, another student, a colleague, a leader in school... someone! Do not struggle alone because asking for help isn't a weakness, it is a strength. To struggle on alone will likely end in stress, feeling like a failure and ultimately a desire to leave the classroom. If yourself in a position where you feel you have no support then please contact me and I will help in any way I can.

Plan "easy" lessons for yourself every now and then.

Plan lessons into your week where there is little or no need for you to stand and talk to the class. Facilitate, set them off and allow them the freedom to work independently. Take the time this allows you to carry out interventions, mark books, give verbal feedback and any other jobs you feel that you don't have time to do. This is allowed… it is part of the job you are paid to do…

In my early career I felt like this was cheating. I wondered how more experienced colleagues could arrive later and go home far earlier than me and seem to achieve better results in the classroom. Timetable management. Use the time you are in school as efficiently as possible.

Work smarter not harder.

Find ways of saving yourself time. Working harder is not as effective as working smarter. For example, when you collect in children's books, ask them to hand them in open on the page they have been working on. If you save 10 seconds a book in a class of 30 then that is 5 minutes extra where you would have been flicking through pages. Train children to do jobs in the classroom like organise resources, tidy the reading corner, collect and hand out books. Every minute you save yourself is an extra minute you can dedicate to other jobs or, ideally, your own wellbeing.

Only be concerned about the things you can control – don't waste energy on things you can't.

There are many things in education that you have no control over but many of these things seem to cause teachers the most stress. For example, OFSTED… "The Call" is something that is talked about constantly. For the first few years of my career I was constantly concerned about it (and had it every year). I wasted so much energy and brain time on thinking about it but I could not control when it would happen. Instead, I should have concentrated on making sure my day to day practice was as good as possible for the benefit of my children. I can control (on the whole) what happens in my classroom. I can control the standards and expectations I accept. I can control the quality of work I am willing to accept from my pupils. I can control planning engaging and interesting learning sequences. I can control my positive persona. I can control eating breakfast and lunch. I can control many things, too many things to worry about the things I can't control.

If you take care of everything that is under your control and do it really well then anything you can't control will never have a negative effect on you.

Take at least one day off at the weekend.

I believe you should take both days off at the weekend, however, it is very rare that I am able to do this. As a student and NQT, I worked 7 days a week and then most of half terms and end of term breaks. I felt I had to. Before I began teaching, I played semi-professional rugby on a Saturday, trained twice a week and went to the gym. I could not sustain this as a student teacher and I threw my entire existence into being a teacher. I stopped everything and I regret it. I piled on weight through becoming sedentary, drinking more and eating when I could. You need to make sure that you are working to enable you to have a life and not living to work. What is the point of slogging your guts out if you do not step back and take some time to enjoy your life. Promise yourself to have at least one day off a week; it will make a dramatic difference to your wellbeing.

Plan things to look forward to.

I struggle to focus on more than one thing at once – I always have. For years, I was so focussed on teaching that a holiday would arrive and I would have no plans at all and they would pass by so quickly and then I would be back on the teaching treadmill.

The best holidays are those that are full of the things that you can't do during term time. Make the most of the holidays, they are a much needed (and one of the few) perks of being a teacher. The hard days and weeks are easier to manage when you know that in a few weeks you have amazing adventures to look forward to.

On short days where you arrive and leave in the dark – get outside in the light at some point.

During winter, you travel to work in the dark and generally leave after dark. If you don't leave your classroom all day then it is realistic that you won't go outside in the daylight at all. It can make such a significant difference if you get out into the fresh air and light because you could end up not seeing light all week. Make time to get outside.

Exercise as much as possible.

I remember a lecture about wellbeing during my training. The speaker said, "Even though it is really hard, I try to get to the gym or go for a run every day." I thought that would be no problem as I had an active lifestyle... how wrong I was. Entering the classroom consumed every waking moment and my active lifestyle disappeared – for many years. It is natural to become focussed on your own development as a teacher and the progress of your classes but you are a more effective professional if you spend time maintaining your health. Get outside, go for a walk, go for a run, go to the gym ... do something. It might seem like wasted time but it really isn't.

Leave early once a week.

Your school caretaker should not have to ask you to pack up and leave everyday but I got into a routine where this was the case. I had several TeachFirst trainee colleagues who were locked in their buildings because the caretaker missed them on their final rounds. Don't let this happen to you. Plan an evening a week where you leave school by four o'clock. Plan a low/no preparation lesson for the following day and enjoy your evening of freedom. Refresh, reset and recharge. A few hours away from the grind of teaching will do wonders for your wellbeing.

You will lose your voice.

I generally lose my voice at some point in Autumn term. I start with a slightly sore throat which then gets worse and worse. The ironic thing is that when my voice does go completely the pain seems to go too... I just can't speak. I am rubbish at treating myself and always try to push through the initial sore throat. Your voice is your job... look after it. Don't push through and carry on as normal. Plan lessons where you do not have to do much talking. Speak gently and quietly. Make sure you medicate and consume any wonderful family recipes you may have... and if you can, speak to your leadership and explain your situation – if they are sensible then they will help you manage because if you lose your voice they will have to replace you for a number of days. Look after yourself.

Take a break from school work during the holidays.

I used to look forward to holidays as it gave me a chance to catch up on all the work I had not managed to do and I always intended to get loads done so I was ahead for the following term. I also gave myself the treat of saving my academic assignments for these teaching breaks. Then I would decide to have a couple of days off and feel guilty the whole time.

If you can get to the point of doing no work in your holidays then you are better than me. I now plan a day (sometimes a day and a half) that I dedicate to work. I haven't worked out whether this is better at the very start or the very end of the holidays but either way I plan it, speak to my family and we all know that is when I will be working. It means I have several consecutive days where I do not do anything school related... this is essential because by the end of each half term I am unbelievably tired. I find my brain can't hold information and even the simplest task becomes insanely difficult. You must recharge and relax or you will burnout. You must step off the treadmill... take a well-deserved break – you've earnt it.

Mark in lessons as much as possible.

Written marking is a much-debated topic in education and schools have a variety of marking policies. Sadly, there are many who treat marking as a way of showing progress to external visitors (OFSTED, school improvement officers, consultants etc) and not for the benefit of the children. Written marking takes a long time and often has no impact on learning. As a student and NQT my school's policy required the use of green and pink highlighters for different areas and three written comments in the form of two stars and a wish... for every... single... piece... of... work! I had no idea how to manage this (and still don't know if anyone could or did). I had 36 children in my class, they had 3 books each that was 108 books to mark. If I managed to take 3 minutes per book (an impossible task) then this meant marking would take 324 minutes per night... over 5 hours per night... WHAT! There were ways of avoiding this, like staggering which books I got the children to do written work in each day but when one set of books takes well over an hour to mark the task is ridiculous.

My pivotal moment came when following a conversation of Twitter about teachers' favourite soundtracks to mark to. Classical, musicals, pop, country and many other genres were mentioned until a single post exploded into my life... **"I mark to the sound of children working around me."** The biggest impact you can have is marking with children and giving them "live and immediate" feedback. Writing a comment, as you drink wine and watch tv has little or no effect on their learning. You can drown in written marking, do not let this happen.

The things I wish I knew about...

Home Life

You will start correcting your loved one's grammar and setting them questions in random situations.

The world becomes your classroom but it is important to step out of teacher mode. There is no better way to annoy your family and friends than talking to them like a pupil. "Don't patronise me, I'm not one of your pupils."

I also find I can never miss an opportunity for learning in real life situations but I'm sure my wife does not need to work out: "I have bought 24 of these and it cost me £18, how many would 12 of them cost?" and so on and so forth.

Let your grown-up family and friends off the hook... they've done their education and if they want to speak with incorrect grammar, then let them... (no matter how much it kills you inside). Or do what I do and correct them with your tongue firmly inserted in your cheek.

Every shop, outing, gameshow etc will make you think "that would be a great lesson".

It becomes impossible to visit anywhere without thinking about how great this or that would be for a lesson. Be prepared... it happens. Try to enjoy yourself at the same time and shut off from your teacher self.

Keep going with your hobbies no matter how hard this may seem.

I spoke about playing rugby earlier in the book and how this ended when I began teaching. Hobbies are an essential part of your life and what makes you the person you are. It is possible to be a great teacher and still do the things you love... in fact it is essential that you do. How can you tell your children to dream and achieve anything they want to do if you are not taking your own advice? It might be that you must do them less often or in a less formal way, or at a lower standard (with lower pressure) but please don't let your hobbies disappear completely. It took me 6 years to get back into rugby and they are 6 years I will never, ever get back.

Stay in touch with your friends.

I'm sure you have the message by now, teaching is all consuming. You focus everything you have on becoming excellent and nothing else matters. This was the case for me and sadly I allowed myself to fall out of touch with many close friends. I missed the odd call here and there and then forgot to ring them back or reply to a text message or group chat. I missed the odd get together here and there until I found myself in a position where they didn't even bother asking anymore because they knew I would say no or not even respond. Your network and support system is essential to your wellbeing and to your eventual success as a teacher. Make the effort to stay in touch with your friends, be honest with them about when you are too busy but make sure that when you do have time that you dedicate some of it to them.

Make time for your family.

For the first three years of my teaching career my fiancé (now wife) called me "Mr Toshiba head." My school issued laptop was a Toshiba and this is what she saw in front of my face, most of the time. I know have a two-year-old daughter who I am determined will call me daddy and not "Mr Laptop Head."

Your pupils are important, of course they are but so are your family. My mum, a retired teacher, still tells the story about an evening many years ago, when she was working late planning for school - my brother and I stated... "You love those children more than us."

Pupils move on and grow up and more than likely will hold you in their very distant memories but your family are here to stay! Enjoy them, give them the time they deserve! After all, who are you working so hard for?

Listen to your body and look after yourself.

Your body is excellent at self-regulating... listen to it! If you are tired, sleep. If you are hungry, eat. If you are thirsty, drink. Too often we ignore our bodies to the point of making ourselves ill. It is essential that we all take responsibility to look after ourselves. Too many teachers run themselves into the ground and have to take extended periods off work and even leave the profession. This applies to both physical and mental health – nothing is worth making yourself ill for. Listen to your body and look after yourself. You only get one life so make sure you are living it!

Make lunches in advance.

Eating lunch and having a drink is an important part of every day at work. It is far too easy to work right through and get to the end of the day starving, with a terrible headache because you have had nothing to eat or drink. Take a water bottle to work and make sure you are drinking regularly. Make healthy lunches the night before so all you have to do is grab your box from the fridge (you will save time and money doing this). Take a break at lunchtimes and spend time in the staffroom to eat and recharge for the afternoon session.

You will experience "Sunday fear."

No matter how prepared you are for a Monday, you will experience Sunday fear. This is just part of the job. You will question whether you are prepared and go through all the things that might go wrong on a Monday... Have I forgotten something? Will so and so trash the classroom? Will this endless pile of books be marked? Why am I doing this? Then you arrive on Monday morning and everything is absolutely fine. Push through people, you are doing an excellent job!

The things I wish I knew about...

Wider School Life

Don't fear parents.

Parents are part of school life and in general they are fiercely supportive of their children. It is your job to communicate with them. This communication is much easier if you have a relationship with them so get outside at the start and end of the day. Say hello and have conversations with them. Make sure you are giving positive messages whenever possible. Try not to let the first time you speak to them be when you have to call them to tell them that their child has done something wrong.

You won't always have the support of parents and at times you will have difficult conversations but if they understand that everything you are doing is in the best interest of their child then it will be fine in the long run. Don't fear parents, you all want the best for the children.

Get to know children from all year groups. Learn names as quickly as possible.

"Young lady." "Young lad." "Excuse me." "Oi." Are nowhere near as effective as effective as – "John, no thank you." "Amber, walking please." "Imran, thank you so much for holding that door. How is your brother doing?"

The quicker you learn names, the quicker you can build relationships and have a wider presence through school. Everything becomes easier when you know names and have relationships with as many pupils as possible. It is the brief conversations in corridors, dinner hall and the playground that can make your life easier in the long term. Take advantage of the chances you get to lay your foundations with each child. Find out bits of information about them, their family and their interests and ask them about it each time you see them. If you remember things about them then they will know you genuinely care and then they in turn will begin to genuinely care about what you are asking them to do.

Play the long game (before long that child who you ignored might be the one you have to win over in your class).

Teach children to play with each other.

You will get frustrated with the amount of issues you inherit from breaks and lunchtimes. "So and so called me this." "He kicked my ball away." "I wanted to go in goal but they wouldn't let me."

It is natural to blame the adults on duty for not dealing with situations (and sometimes this is true) however, more often and not, issues arise because children have no idea how to play together during an unstructured half an hour. It is worth your time to model how to play. Give them strategies to deal with various situations. TEACH them over and over again. This is an important part of social development and is very much part of education. The amount of time you will save in the long run with children coming in from breaks and lunchtimes calm, settled and happy is worth the investment.

Don't moan about things – try to find a solution.

Things go wrong in schools. Fact. When they do you have a choice: moan about it and allow it to keep going wrong or find a solution. Far too often I have witnessed the same conversation repeated in staffrooms – "It's happened again. That happened yesterday as well. I knew that was going to happen."

FIX IT THEN. This is a simplistic view but it is too easy to blame other people when perhaps being more proactive would be better.

Celebrate out of school success.

Children do not all leave the building and play PlayStation all night then come back to school. Many are doing excellent and wonderful things – whether this is a piece of work they have decided to do because they loved a lesson you taught or winning a national taekwondo tournament. It is too easy to pay these things lip service but is this not exactly what we are encouraging? "Chase your dreams, you can do anything you believe in, be excellent." Encourage children to tell you things they are doing and make a MASSIVE deal about it.

All staffrooms have underlying politics – be careful.

Some schools have mug and seat politics, others do not. Be careful before you use someone's treasured mug and sit in someone else's seat they have used for twenty years. My advice is to ask on your first day and then spend some time learning the culture of your school. It is very easy to annoy people without realising.

When I was a student I felt that the staff were being quite cold and stand offish with me and it turns out that I had been introduced as the head teacher's friend from rugby (we had never met before). They all thought I was there to spy on them and as a result it took me a long time to feel part of the staff.

Morale in a school is essential – do your best to keep yours and others high.

It is palpable when morale is low in a school and the atmosphere is not nice for anybody. Many different factors can contribute to low morale but you can make a difference by staying positive. If you can look after your own wellbeing and bring a smile and positive mindset to school, you will be able to raise the morale of all those around you – including more experienced colleagues.

Positivity can make an immediate and long-lasting impact within a school. Be the shining light.

Children and adults get tired towards the end of half terms.

Teaching is hard. Half terms are long and relentless. Everyone in a school is human (including leaders) and everyone gets very tired towards the end of each half term. People are more stressed, children find it harder to behave, teachers' patience is running thin, standards and expectations can slip, and everyone is at breaking point. It genuinely feels like you a crawling towards a break sometimes.

As a result, staff members become more fractious and cracks can appear. Time seems to be shorter and there always seems to be more to do. I suggest keeping this in mind when communicating with colleagues and leaders at this time of year. Does the conversation you want have to happen at that point or can it wait until after the break when everyone is refreshed and recharged?

There will be trends that appear and may make no sense to you.

Trends are as old as education itself – I imagine conkers was the historic version of fidget spinners. When I was at school it was marbles and Pogs. More recent trends include loom bands and slime. Then there is flossing and dabbing where children breakout into strange jerking movements in what seems like an involuntary spasm. I suggest you use trends to your advantage – link learning to them and you will have your children hooked from the moment you give them the title. I can't wait to see what occurs next (and kind of hope I invent it).

Have a system to remember numerous passwords and logins.

You will have many passwords, logins and websites to use. You will also be required to change your password regularly. There are many occasions that I changed my password and then had no idea what it was the next time I tried to login. Trying to reset passwords takes time. Time is the most precious thing in teaching and wasting it is very frustrating. Have a system and stick to it (save yourself time).

Be on time for assembly...

Be on time for everything. There is nothing worse than an entire school waiting for you and your class. Avoid the embarrassment and make sure you set off earlier than you think you need to. It is better to be first into the hall than last because you do not want to be blamed for children missing time from their break or staff not getting their coffee because assembly over ran.

Be on time for duties.

Make sure you are on time for any duties you have. If you are late then you leave a colleague on their own, or worse, a group of children unsupervised. If something happens when you should have been there then you are responsible for this – not a good situation to be in if you are being blamed for something that was preventable. Also, colleagues will be frustrated if you constantly leave them short staffed because they have to work harder than they should have to.

The things I wish I knew about...

Behaviour Management

Never, ever, ever reward poor behaviour – children remember.

Children choose poor behaviour for many different reasons. Your school will have a policy and you must stick to this as consistently as you can. Children need to know the outcome of their behaviour. Having rewards in class is a great tool, but only if you use them to enforce the behaviour you want to see. Too many times you see a child causing havoc and then being great in the ten minutes before a reward and still receiving it. That child gets the message that it is ok to do whatever they want all week and just turn it on in the run up to a reward. The other children get the message that they don't need to make the right decisions either because they can turn it on just before the reward as well. If you do this regularly you will lose your class and that is a terrible position to be in.

I had a child who was struggling to make the right choices in school, there were clear reasons why but these were not an excuse for the violence and language he was choosing. One afternoon, after a particularly challenging lunchtime he had been in crisis and was not ready to return to class. I and the other children needed a break so I organised for him to go to another class to help some younger children. This was great for that afternoon but I saw a pattern develop where he would ask to go to that class, be told no, then appear to go into crisis before asking to go to that class again. It was my mistake of rewarding the initial bad choices that had messaged to him that the way to get that reward again was to make the same poor choices. Never again will I knowingly reward poor choices, there are too many children making the right choices all the time who deserve the rewards.

Make sure you recognise your always children.

It is far too easy to overlook and take the children, who ALWAYS make the right choices, for granted. I have been guilty of this over the years. Just because they always do the right thing and try their hardest doesn't mean they don't deserve recognition and reward for it – in fact they probably deserve it more than those children who only make the right choices for short periods of time.

Always think, what message am I giving the children by doing this. For example: Child A: always makes the right choices, is polite and tries their best every day. Child B: rarely makes the right choice, is often rude and only tries their best on occasion. You have a certificate to hand out in assembly for "star of the week". Child A has been their normal self all week. Child B has also been themselves except on Wednesday where they were polite and produced some excellent work. On Thursday they were great all morning and produced some more impressive work. Thursday lunchtime they refused to follow the instructions given by another member of staff and were very rude to a group of children from your class.

Too often the certificate would be given to Child B because the teacher wanted to reinforce the behaviour from Wednesday and Thursday Morning. What is truly being reinforced is the fact that it is ok to only try sometimes and it is acceptable to be rude to staff and other children because you get rewarded anyway for small amounts of effort. Surely Child A should get the reward for displaying the desired behaviour all week? This would reinforce the expectation of excellence at all times. Always consider the message you are giving and the expectations you want to set in your classroom.

Understand that there are reasons for poor behaviour but these are not excuses.

Behaviour is somebody's way of telling you something that they can't put into words. There are many reasons why children choose to misbehave and I have always tried to look past the behaviour to the person behind it. Whilst addressing the underlying issues it is important never to excuse unacceptable behaviours because of them. Rules are rules and they are there for a reason, the same is true of society and the rule of law. Police will not overlook a crime because the person in question has "stuff going on at home." As the teacher you must challenge all behaviour consistently, reward those who deserve it and give consequences out to those who deserve them.

Behaviour management is an ongoing battle, especially in extreme cases. It is the culmination of hours of conversations, the ability to build trust and a mutual respect between you and the other person. There are many times you will come across a child who makes your days horrible because they are lashing out or can't access education because they have fallen behind their peers. Talk to them, find out what is going on, put things in place to help but NEVER accept anything from them that you wouldn't from another child. In the long run, it is the only fair thing to do for the child or they will get a shock as they grow older when they experience strict and lasting consequences for their poor choices.

You do not need to shout.

I used to think I had to show my commanding dominance and instil fear and trepidation into my pupils... I was wrong. Fear is not a good emotion to have in a school. Respect is far more powerful. If you are consistent, build relationships, ensure that fairness is applied in all situations, don't ever accept less than their best and set your expectations very high, then pupils will respect you and your authority (although it may not always feel like it). If you get to the point of shouting then you have lost control... you know it and worst of all the children know it.

Personally, if I had a colleague or boss who shouted at me every time I made a mistake, I would not have any respect for them at all. I may do as they ask but I would not feel comfortable to go above and beyond or try new things. I would also actively seek to leave their company.

Second, now I have my beautiful daughter, I would never accept any person on this planet shouting at her in the way I have heard some teachers shout at their pupils. Treat your pupils the way you would expect someone to treat your own children.

Finally, we all have animal instincts of fight or flight – being shouted at immediately raises adrenaline and triggers these innate reactions. I have seen a range of responses to shouting (none positive). Shouting and swearing back at the shouting adult; chair throwing; trying to climb out of a window (first or second floor); running away (slamming the classroom door or not); tears; standing and taking it in silence; completely shutting down and refusing to move; and my least favourite – mocking laughter.

I am not in the slightest saying overlook poor behaviour. In fact, the very opposite. Part of our job is to address these things but also teach why it is wrong. Rather than shouting, use a calm, assertive tone, state the issue and any consequence for the actions. Do not get dragged into arguments (children are wizards at drawing you in).

If you are consistent and fair over a period of time then you will win the respect of your children and behaviour will improve because the message you are calmly giving is: I will not allow you to make poor behaviour choices and if you do then you will always get a consequence.

I suggest you spend the money and read the most wonderful 'Behaviour' book I have ever read (so many eye openers and light bulb moments) – 'When the Adults Change, Everything Changes' (by Paul Dix).

The things I wish I knew about...

Classroom Teaching

Maslow's hierarchy of needs is essential for students and staff.

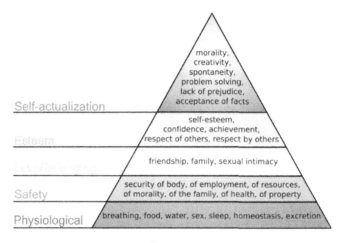

Source:
https://simple.wikipedia.org/wiki/Hierarchy

To allow children to learn it is essential to ensure they are in the mind space to do so. There are many needs that should be taken care of at home, that for too many children, are not. Try forcing a child to learn who hasn't slept, had no breakfast and may be getting evicted from their house and you will most likely not get the response you desire. Similarly, try teaching a week when you haven't eaten properly, stayed up until midnight planning, are worried about your performance in an observation, fallen out with your partner and feel like you are underperforming - there is no chance you will perform at your best. Maslow's hierarchy is the basis for understanding and achieving exceptional

performance for children and teachers alike –
make sure you get it right.

Know that to your children you are a superhero.

You are a constant in all your children's lives.
They may not tell you but they really appreciate
everything you do for them, even when they
seem to be on a mission to do the opposite of
everything you ask. Keep being the constant
and never let them get away with anything less
than their best.

Don't be scared to give children their say.

It is not a weakness to allow children to have
their say. It does not have to be your way or the
high way. Imagine a meeting where you are
blamed for doing something wrong by one of
your managers. Imagine if in this meeting you
were not given any opportunity to give your side
of the story. This would lead to frustration and
resentment towards your manager.

I have found that when children are given the
opportunity to have their say, they are more
honest and it defuses a situation quickly. A
good question I have asked is – what do you
think the fair thing is to happen now? More
often than not, the child will say the

consequence you were going to give anyway. Sometimes they will say a consequence that is wildly disproportionate to the incident and you can manage this however you see fit.

Activate children as learners.

Similar to above, give children their say about their learning. You can guide them towards the topics you need to cover but if they feel they have had a choice then they will be more invested. Learning is a journey you should go on together, not something you do to the children. Children have fantastic ideas and it is exciting to follow them through to fruition.

Be creative.

There is not one way to teach something. Creativity is a fantastic way of engaging children in their learning. Using songs, raps, pictures and drama to help children learn knowledge is a great tool. Keeping things varied and creative also supports engagement from children – I'll never forget an English lesson where I asked them to paint a landscape from a description in the Last Wild (Piers Torday) – the response was "Art in English sir, you're mad!" The work they produce was phenomenal!

Make the most of every learning minute.

Like I keep saying, time is precious. If you waste 5 minutes a day, that is 25 minutes a week, that is 150 minutes in a 6-week half term, that is 300 minutes a term, 900 minutes a year. That's 15 hours of lost learning time (over 2 full school days) over the course of one year. Imagine if that 5 minutes was 10, or 20 or longer!

You can weave learning into periods that would otherwise be dead time. Tidying up, you can have a times table song playing or be reading to the class. Lining up, you can ask children quickfire questions or get them to ask each other questions. Take every opportunity you can to fill every possible second with learning – it will make an enormous difference in the long run.

Remember that small improvements everyday make massive improvements over time – tell the children.

I have always felt that I need to be much better at things immediately and if I'm not then I never will be. The children I have taught will also feel like this – "I don't know my 7 times table so I never will."

I had an epiphany this year and it links to weight loss. As I said earlier, when I started teaching I led an active lifestyle and weighed about 16.5stones, ran the Great North Run in just over 2 hours without stopping and played semi-professional rugby in the National Leagues. 6 years into my career and I had piled on 4 stones, couldn't run to the end of my street and played no sport at all. I turned 30 and decided that this had to change. I sorted my diet out, stopped drinking, started going to the gym and joined my local rugby club. I lost 6 lbs in my first week of diet and training. I was ecstatic... this was going to be easy! The following week I put on 2 lbs... WHAT! I wanted to lose 56lbs (4 stones) but it seemed like too big of a mountain to climb. It was at this point I read a blog about weight loss and it made a point that had never really clicked in my brain – If I lost 1lb per week for a year then I would lose 52lbs or just under 4 stones. This would take me nearly to my goal. 1lb does not sound like a lot and is certainly a manageable amount to lose in a week but long term, with consistent effort I would be back to where I wanted to be. I am now nearly 40lbs lighter and playing semi-pro rugby again.

The same can be applied to learning. Children see things as the mountain – times tables are an example. If you learn all the times tables up to 12x12 by heart there are 144 facts to recall. If you also learn the division facts that go alongside this (e.g. 4 x 3 = 12 so 12 / 4 = 3 and 12 / 3 = 4) then it raises to 432 facts. Can you blame children for thinking they will never be able to learn these? What if they learnt one times table and the corresponding division facts per day? That is only 3 things to learn and embed and after 144 days then they would know everything. 3 facts are a lot less scary than 432. It is your job as a teacher to break huge, massive, scary concepts down into manageable, bitesize chunks. Make things seem as easy as possible and let all our pupils know it is a journey we must go on before we get to the destination and it is ok not to know everything straight away.

Celebrate successes for all children.

Children work hard and want to do well. They deserve to celebrate when they have success. Let them share their work with other members of staff and each other. Let them read it out. Put it up on display. Read it out in assembly. Send the message of – when you succeed, we are very proud and want to tell everyone about it.

Set your expectations higher than you ever thought you could.

If you expect poor standard work with low level vocabulary and spelling mistakes and poor handwriting then that is exactly what you get. If you expect exceptional work, with unbelievable vocabulary, perfect spelling and beautiful handwriting (and don't accept anything less) then this is exactly what you will get. Children will raise their games as high as you set the bar. It might take some time for them to hit your standards but they will. Do not lower them and do not allow them to not meet them.

Don't accept anything less than children's best.

Children will get away with anything they can. If they can hand in work that is sub-standard then they will and why wouldn't they. You must be the bastion against this, the last line of defence against lack of effort. Send the message that if it is less than their best then it will be done again. It won't take long for them to realise that it is easier to do it great first time than have to re-write it again to the acceptable standard. This is hard to stay on top of but if you don't then your children will fall short of where they should be – it is worth the extra effort. You work very hard to plan and resource creative and interesting lessons so why should your children not have to work hard to produce their best too?

Get routines set up early and rehearse.

Routines make your life so much easier! Children perform best when they know what you expect of them in different situations and when they know what is happening when. I have found that some children really struggle with change, so moving an assembly, or over running on a lesson can be enough to cause unwanted behaviours because those children are basically saying "I haven't got a clue what is going on, I know I should be in English but its Maths but I did Maths earlier but it's still going on... What do I do? HELP!"

At one of my schools, we always finished the day with a story. One day, I had to move story time to the very start of the day. After I finished, I noticed one of my pupils grabbing his lunch box and lining up at the door. "Where do you think you're going?" I asked. "It's home time sir, you read our story." This boy had been in school for 15 minutes and he was so used to the end of day routine he believed he was out of there.

Plan routines like you would plan lessons. This is something I overlooked during my student and most of my NQT years and my classroom management suffered because of it. Some of the things I have found most useful are:

Lining up order (written and placed next to the door) – this gives no room for arguments or falling out over pushing in and so forth. Change it every half term. Whenever you line up and wherever you are make sure they are in lining up order – you will avoid so many unnecessary arguments.

Activity on entry – children with nothing to do will find ways to entertain themselves: chatting, play fighting, climbing, throwing things and many more things an unprepared classroom offers. ALWAYS have something for children to do upon entry to the room and train them to do it. An activity on the board, a problem on their table, read in silence... whatever it is you expect make it routine and do it every single day. Smooth starts to each session of learning make the whole session easier. Manic starts mean you are fighting fires from the first second and you will feel yourself losing control. Also, if you embed the routine and do it every day then there are no excuses children can give for not settling and getting on straight away... "I didn't know what to do." "Really? We did it yesterday, and the day before, and the day before that."

Allocate children individual classroom jobs – in general, children love them. Activate them to take ownership of their classroom and train them how to do it. 30 children doing one job each saves one tired teacher doing 30 jobs at the end of the day.

Assembly places – again, no room for arguments and falling out and avoids chatty friends sitting together. Take a list with you and make it obvious you are checking otherwise these well-planned seats tend to be 'accidentally forgotten about'.

Wet break routine –in Britain, these happen a lot! Make sure you have a plan, some prepared resources/games and set rules. Practise these and before long when the heavens open you can just say "Indoor break guys," and they will just sort themselves out… once getting over the devastation of not getting to play football or run around with their friends.

There are many more techniques that you will discover and some schools may have these written into policy, but the five above are the most significant ones I wish I had known and used from day 1 in my classroom.

Always fully investigate any complaints from children.

You will get lots of complaints and allegations every single day –

"She called me this."

"He did this to me."

"She's throwing X, Y or Z."

It is far too easy to skim over these as annoyances and I have done this many times using the go to phrases:

"Just stay away from him/her."

"Just ignore them."

"I'm watching."

Then continue teaching or patrolling on your duty. It may feel like the situation is over and you have placated the child in question but this can lead to issues down the line: children taking revenge as they feel aggrieved; angry phone calls from parents who feel nothing was done; or worst of all accusations of bullying. Do not let small incidents fester because they can soon become big issues when they really did not need to. Make sure you fully investigate and make sure the wronged child sees you doing it. Don't wade in all guns blazing to the accused, ask questions like:

"Why do you think X might be upset?"

"Can you tell me what happened with Y?

"I'm not accusing you but I need you to tell me why Z has just come to tell me they are upset."

For more extreme situations, find out everyone who witnessed the event, speak to all involved and make notes. It is better to be overly thorough and have notes and statements than be caught out later. It has happened to me and it feels awful when something you thought was innocuous actually led to a child going home and breaking down in tears. Be proactive, get stuff sorted, nip issues in the bud and let all children see that you are... it might seem like a waste of time but it WILL save you time later. It will also help you build better relationships and gain the children's trust/respect as they will feel listened to, valued and believed.

Spend time with your quiet non-attention seeking children.

I have heard these described as "Grey children," because they blend in. It is important to share your time fairly between all your children because they all deserve it. Just because they don't shout out, throw chairs or stamp their feet doesn't mean they shouldn't have your time. It is difficult because attention-seekers do attract your attention and it is easier to gravitate to them but remember that all your children only get one shot at their education and all deserve as much of you as possible.

If you give children who are behind low level work with low expectations - when will they catch up?

One of the most poignant takes I know on this comes from an episode of The Simpsons where Bart is put into a 'catch up' group. The teacher draws a lower-case a on the black board and says, "Ok, everyone take out your safety pencil and circles of paper... This week I hope we can finish our work on the later A." Bart claps his hands over his eyes and says, "Let me get this straight. We are behind the rest of our class and we are going to catch up by going slower than them... Cuckoo!" And it is cuckoo isn't it. Let's looks at an example: A child falls behind in Y1 and hasn't embedded everything necessary to access all the Y2 curriculum so the Year 2 teacher gives them Year 1 work and eventually simplified Year 2 work whilst the rest of the class are working through the entire year 2 curriculum. When that child starts Year 3 and hasn't accessed much of the year 2 curriculum they are now a year behind the rest of their peers. If this continues throughout their school career then they will always be at least a year behind and this soon leads to avoidance techniques such as poor behaviour or low attendance.

In my opinion, the most skilled teachers set high expectations for all children and then scaffold their learning to get them all to the same point. Children are very shrewd and will pick up quickly if they are not doing the same level work as others. I find honesty works very well... for example, "We both know that you are finding it difficult to decode the words when reading but your reading skills are as good as everyone else's. Let's work really hard together on the decoding and soon you will be great at all of reading." Keep checking in with them and highlight their great progress: "Wow, remember two weeks ago when you couldn't tell me your 6 times table and now you know them all. That's amazing. Next challenge is..."

These children may have struggled for years and felt like they are "rubbish" and "not as clever as the other children". You need to show them their wins and keep pushing them.

Fun is an essential part of learning.

I have been to many meetings or training sessions where the facilitator stands at the front and talks for hours. I find myself shutting off, day dreaming, doodling or staring out the window... and I'm a grown-up professional with a well-developed attention span. I have also attended great meetings and training sessions where the facilitator has included activities, opportunities to move, sections to discuss with others and regular breaks/games. I always leave the active sessions feeling I have learnt more and have been more engaged.

Children have much shorter attention spans so bear the above in mind when planning learning sequences. Keep them engaged, active and interested.

Children need to move so if you can make a lesson involve movement - do.

I mentioned the importance of this in the above section but I want to give an example here. Let's take a reading session where you are looking at an extract and ask a question with a true or false response. You could ask the children to write a T or F on a whiteboard and hold it up. You could ask them to put their thumbs up or down. You could even ask them to write their answer in their book. These options are legitimate ways of addressing this problem but I would challenge you to get some movement in here – it not only helps the children stay focussed but helps you to assess them quickly and, even better, not have to mark anything.

You could have a true poster on one wall and a false poster on the other and ask them to go and stand next to their choice. For even less preparation time (none), you could just tell them that one area of the room is true and another area is false. Once they have moved to their choice, you can question further and ask them to justify why they moved to their current position. This helps you assess but also lets them know that you could ask any of them at any point so they all need a response prepared and can't just follow their friends. This technique also works with agree/disagree, A, B, C, D and many more question types in all subjects. I will explore many more activities to help you save time, assess and secure progress in your classroom in my next book 'The things I wish I had known about Active Assessment'.

Set expectations for everything and stick to them.

You may know what you want and expect but if you do not constantly remind them then the children will not know. If you want a silent line with gaps between children then tell them this and model exactly how you want them to stand. Do it repeatedly until it is second nature. If you only tell them once then it is not fair for you to expect them to remember the next time. Be very specific – if you want silent say "Silent," and explain what this means. If you say, "I need a quiet line, thank you." Do not be surprised if you get some noise because quiet doesn't mean silent.

If you want a piece of work presented in a certain way, make one yourself and show the children. Model absolutely everything, act things out, break things down into single step instructions. Be clear and repeat, repeat, repeat and never compromise. Children WILL meet your expectations whether they are low or high so set them higher than you think possible.

Children need to be taught how to remember things.

Remembering things and recalling facts or strategies is a skill we take for granted as adults because we have had years of practice. The phrase, "In one ear and out of the other," is true unless we specifically teach recall techniques. Being honest with the children and making it clear that they must remember what you are about to tell them is a good start – then ask them about it later to show them you were not kidding. There are many techniques to help memory and it is important these are interwoven into the curriculum. Too many times I have heard teachers say, "They just can't remember stuff." I always think, have we taught them how to or given the knowledge the status it deserves to be remembered? I would bet a lot of money that the same children who, "Can't remember stuff," could recite their favourite song lyrics word for word perfect, or every member of their favourite football team, or the name of every "skin" on Fortnite or every single cheat for a computer game. They remember these things because they matter to them and are highly relevant. It is our jobs as teachers to make the skills and knowledge we teach them MATTER and be highly relevant.

Have a consistent answer to "Can I go to the toilet?"

Find out the school policy. If there isn't one then create a classroom policy. You will be asked this question at least 3000 times a day so be prepared. Personally, I would never have a blanket "No" policy because I would never want a child to be uncomfortable or worse, in pain but you will also have children who push you on this rule because they want a break from the classroom. My favourite has been, "Ask me again in five minutes if you still need to go." I find that the ones who just wanted a break tend to forget that they were desperate for the toilet and the ones who really need to go come and ask again. Another colleague instigated a "once in a session rule," where pupils can go to the toilet once during lessons in the morning and once in the afternoon. This made the regular askers have to really choose when they actually needed to go rather than repeatedly asking you.

Whatever your policy, stick to it (but be human as well – sometimes children genuinely need to go, may be ill or have medical/psychological reasons to go).

Have plan Bs ready for early finishers.

Have things ready for those children who finish activities quickly – there will always be some who will always fly through.

I remember one occasion where I set a very challenging maths investigation and fully expected it to take at least one lesson if not two to fully investigate before revealing the solution. After 47 seconds one boy put his hand up and proudly announced, "finished." I checked his solution and he had nailed it. It was just one of those things that he could just see and didn't really know how. I had no plan B prepared and it took me a few minutes (which I should really have been spending with the other children on the investigation) to find him an extension activity.

As you gain more experience it becomes easier to create extensions of learning or deepening tasks but I would suggest that you build a bank of go to, meaningful, tasks that you can direct children to once they have finished. Also, if you find yourself at a loss give them a reward and allow them to read their favourite book, magazine, newspaper or comic in a comfortable place – after all they have earned it by their phenomenal brilliance.

Prepare hooks for learning.

In my experience, children who absolutely love what they are doing will produce far better work than when they don't really care. Hooking children into their learning is essential. There are many ways to do this: follow their interests and link learning to them; make it real – write letters to real people for real reasons, run an enterprise project with real money; have an end outcome they can be proud of and give a real audience (publish work in books, get it on display, tweet it, Facebook page it, invite parents in to see it, present it in assembly – don't hide it away in an exercise book).

If you are struggling to think of a hook (as we all are at times) find out whatever the current trend is and link the title or first slide to it. It doesn't matter how tenuous it is but "The angles of a perfect dab," is more appealing than "Angles".

Teach motivation.

Motivation is a skill and must be taught. Talking about how to dream and fail and pick themselves up again is essential. The curriculum is incredibly full already but the benefits of spending time on developing motivation are amazing. I have shown the same YouTube videos as I was shown in rugby and American Football training sessions. The impact has been huge both on my pupils' personal development and their work. I suggest you find motivational quotes, passages, videos, film clips, speeches and build these into your classroom practice. It will not be wasted time.

Pride goes a long way.

Hand in hand with motivation is pride. Building a sense of pride in themselves and their work is so important for all children. Certain children may never have had someone consistently tell them that they are proud of them. It may be a slow process as they may not believe you straight away but over time and after you not accepting anything less than their best on numerous occasions, they will go above and beyond to make you proud of them. It is important to also make them proud of each other. Stop everyone and tell them how amazing something is and that they should be really proud. Speak to parents and take work out to show them. Stand up in assembly and shout about how amazing your class has been. Do everything possible to make your children feel that what they are doing is amazing and keep doing it over and over again and they will soon be desperate for that feeling of pride and their effort levels and production will elevate.

Praise is precious.

Praise is one of the most important tools you have as a teacher and will have longer lasting effects than an instant gratification award like chocolate. I believe praise should be part of everyday life in a classroom, however, I think in my early years of teaching I gave it out too freely. Take a chocolate reward – would you give it out for sub-standard effort or outcome? No. Praise should be the same. If you praise work or effort that is less than you expect then you are sending the message that it is ok. If you save your praise for when children have earnt it then it will mean far more and be something they desire.

Effort over outcome.

Professor Carol Dweck led research into fixed vs growth mindset in humans. To paraphrase – a fixed mindset is where someone believes they can or can't do something. "I am good at art." "I'm can't do art."

A growth mindset is where someone believes they can get better at everything through sustained effort and practise.

If you continually praise a child for getting 10/10 on a maths test then they will believe they are good at maths, until they come across a problem that they find challenging. They can actively avoid putting themselves in a challenging situation as they believe the way to be good at maths is to get everything correct. On the other hand, if you praise a child constantly for their effort to get to their outcomes then they will believe the way to be good at something is to try their best and eventually they will get there.

I have found teaching and praising effort over outcome leads to far more resilient learners who eventually produce amazing outcomes because they believe they can.

Basic skills underpin everything

I have been guilty of overlooking this at times. When a child writes three pages of the most amazingly, imaginative prose I have tended to focus on the positives rather than look at the fifteen spelling mistakes, poor handwriting and the odd grammar error. It is essential we as teachers do pick up on the basics from the very start of education because once children have got away with things for years they become a habit, which at some point someone must break. It is easier to get it right from the start.

A recent example of this is the implementation of TTrockstars into my daily timetable (an excellent online programme where children earn coins by answering multiplication questions – as many as possible in a minute). In the past I had got my classes to learn times tables as part of the maths curriculum but not given it massive emphasis. Then I pulled my hair out when it took weeks to teach fractions because their basic knowledge of multiples and factors was not good enough. The class who benefited from TTrockstars and half an hour daily practice flew through fractions (and other multiplication based areas of maths) faster than any class I have every taught.

Getting basic skills nailed, such as handwriting, spelling, basic grammar, times tables, number bonds and division facts, helps teaching and learning but it also helps you as a teacher in observations and work scrutiny sessions. If your books are full of repeated basic errors that are not addressed and improved then this reflects badly on you as a teacher (rightly or wrongly). If your books are full of beautiful and accurate work then this reflects well on you.

Unfortunately, managers, consultants, mentors, OFSTED inspectors, improvement partners and anyone else who is tasked with inspecting work in schools do not have much time to look at children's work and therefore they form judgements very fast. If there are many basic errors then they immediately start thinking negatively whereas if books are accurate, look great and show good production then they start thinking positively.

Be sharp on the basics, have sky high expectations – it will save you a lot of time in the long run.

Avoid sticking lots of worksheets in books.

I have seen teachers fall into this trap on too many occasions. A worksheet can be a useful tool to support learning but there are several issues with them:

1. There are generally no lines on them and if there are lines then they are a different size to what the children are used to. This is difficult for children and leads to lower standards of presentation and a poorer impression in books.

2. Worksheets can be too generic and not address individual needs.

3. It is a huge waste of time finding, printing, trimming, handing out, collecting in, handing back out to make sure names are on, marking and sticking in sheets.

Where possible, present information on the board or on an information sheet and ask children to work directly in books. Worksheets might seem like a time saver but they really aren't.

Children love learning new things – let them.

Even the most challenging children love learning new things (although they may never admit it). If a class is interested in something and want to ask questions then delay whatever activity you had planned and go with the conversation. You do not necessarily have to be the expert on every topic because children also get a lot out of going on the learning journey with you. If possible, don't let rigid plans or timeframes get in the way of learning and prevent you from following inquisitive lines of enquiry through to their fullest end.

Remember that children are experiencing many things for the first time with you – enjoy it with them.

It might be the thirteenth time you have taught World War 2, fractions, a particular book but it is the first time your children are learning about it. Teach it like it is the first time you are doing it (except thirteen times better). If you come across as bored then the children will think it's boring. If you are excited then they will be excited. You are selling learning to them... would you buy something from someone who seemed like they were going through the motions and had no enthusiasm. I think not.

Teach skills in arts or surprisingly children won't improve

Early in my career I was guilty of this for sure and I have seen others who are just as guilty. "My class are rubbish at art."

What skills have you taught them? Did you present an image to them and ask them to recreate it? Or place an object in front of them and ask them to produce a realistic charcoal sketch? Would you give them a maths problem and ask them to solve it with no input at all?

I have discovered, through my own mistakes, that until you teach your children HOW to do certain skills in the arts then they will not improve. It is important that you model (find videos that model if you feel you can't), give feedback, allow children to fail and try again, encourage and provide a range of opportunities for pupils to try. It is not true that you can either do or not do the creative subjects. They can and should be learnt/taught like any other. They are not just for filling time in an afternoon! If you find yourself saying "My class are rubbish at art." Perhaps it's time to look at what teaching and learning is happening during these sessions. For far too long I facilitated creative sessions, stood back and allowed my children to remain at exactly the same ability as they were before the session. Now, I teach skills and the improvement and progress I see is amazing (sorry to any pupils in my early classes, I feel I let you down).

Pencil sharpening is a great procrastination technique.

Get on top of this and have a system. What do you want your children to do if they need a sharp pencil? The obvious answer it to let them sharpen their pencil but I have witnessed children deliberately snap their pencil to avoid working. A pencil should be adequately sharpened within 4 or 5 turns in the sharpener so I am not sure why it can sometimes take up to 5 minutes to sharpen a pencil!

One system I have seen is to have a sharp box (where beautifully sharp pencils wait) and a blunt box (where pupils discard their used pencils). When a pupil needs a sharp pencil, they put their blunt one in the blunt box and immediately take a sharp pencil and continue working. The minimum time is lost and the pupils can run the system themselves. Certain pupils are allocated the job of sharpening the blunt box and transferring them to the sharp box.

Children love jobs...

When I started in education I was surprised by how much children love having a job to do (I have seen this from nursery right through to year 13). If you utilise this properly then it can save you hours each week. I worked with a great teacher once who held a weekly lunchtime "Teacher Club," where willing children eagerly stuck things in books, backed work for display, tidied the library and many more things. They loved it, felt important and it saved my colleague SO MUCH TIME!

It can be tempting to give your challenging children jobs to avoid meltdowns but I suggest you do this with care. All too often a child can be given a job to help them calm down but they love doing jobs so they deliberately 'kick off' to be sent to do "their job." They see it as being rewarded for poor behaviour. Perhaps save jobs for the children who are making the right choices and frame it as a reward for making good choices.

Let children be experts.

It is ok to 'let go' and allow the children to become experts in their learning. If they have particular interests or hobbies then it is likely they will be more knowledgeable than you. When I first started I felt like I had to be the person in the room who knew most about everything. I have learnt over time that this isn't the case – children get a lot out of seeing their peers as experts and it helps them believe that they themselves can also be experts on different subjects. Let them teach you things... they love it. I recently had a child trying to teach me binary code and another about the very specific details of narwhals.

Give them a wider audience.

Children always produce better work when they know it is FOR someone or something. It is human nature and we need to harness this. There are many ways to provide an audience:

1. Other classes in school – "Year 3 are visiting us tomorrow and we will be reading them this work."

2. Head/Deputy head teacher – "I have asked Ms X to come in on Friday because you have

been doing brilliantly and I want you to show her your work."

3. Parents/guardians – have events where pupils invite parents in (get them to write the letters) and show all their recent work. Set up galleries, museums, parties, historical recreations, science shows… anything that makes a special and meaningful reason to create amazing work.

4. Social Media – (make sure you know your school's policy) but posting on twitter, Facebook and other sites provides a huge audience for pupil's work.

5. Websites – there are many websites where you can post pupils work and others from around the world can comment and review. Pobble.com is a great example of this for writing.

6. Contact authors – there are many authors who are very responsive and this helps pupils know that "REAL" people are seeing and commenting on their work or questions.

7. Facetime – set up a facetime conference with another school and share each other's work with other children from another setting. You can facetime anyone, from anywhere (just be prepared for technology to fail you – it often does).

8. Publish work in a class book and put a copy in the school library – it is very powerful to see

children selecting this and reading each other's writing.

There are many other ways to give an audience but these are a few easy ones to start with.

Displays give an amazing sense of pride.

I undervalued displays early in my career and saw them very much as a waste of my precious time because they took me a long time and they never seemed to be as appealing as my colleagues'. It took me a while to see how much impact seeing their work on the wall can have on pupils. Pupils feel valued and very proud of having their work proudly displayed for all to see – it also reinforces your high expectations because you can tell them that you only display work that you know reflects their very best effort. Displays are one of those "extra" tasks that ARE worth the time. Let your class's learning spill out into the corridors, flood cloakrooms and fill any available space. Think of the message you are sending to the pupils – You are brilliant, I'm very proud and want others to see how great you are.

Size matters – why is it on the wall if you can't see it?

I have seen many displays, both in classrooms and corridors, where things are just far too small. If people can't read what is displayed, what was the point in you taking the time to put it up? If you invest your time in a display, make sure it is highly useful and children can read what is up there.

For example – I saw a classroom where the teacher had identified 100 spellings that were relevant to the current topic and displayed these on the working wall... in font size 12. Nobody could use these. It would have been more effective to identify 10 words and display them really large so all the children could use them accurately in their writing. These 10 could have been replaced every couple of days or each week of the topic so the children still experienced all the vocabulary (and read it from where they sat).

Build a bank of activities for those empty 5 minutes that occur every now and then.

It doesn't matter how meticulously you plan, there will always be the odd few minutes here or there that you need to fill. Teach your class some learning games and have these as your go to tactic. My favourites are:

1. Class Champion – all children sit in their chairs and you select one child to be "champion". They go and stand behind another child, who stands up. You ask a question about anything you are learning and the first one to answer is "champion", the other sits down. To engage more pupils, you can tell them that you are going to ask them at random to ask the questions and they must have one ready.

2. Guess the _____ (person, fact, number, place, etc) ____: One child stands at the front. You write a person, fact, number, place on a mini-whiteboard and hold it up behind them. They can ask yes/no questions to narrow down the options until they guess the answer. E.g. Is it an even number? Does it have 3 digits? Is it a multiple of 5?

If you have taught and trained them well these games can begin in seconds and last for as long as you need to fill (within reason). You will build your own bank as you gain more experience but I suggest you start with at least 2 because there is nothing more terrifying than "empty time," as this is where problems can begin.

If they can do something 4 times then challenge them with something.

If you are teaching a concept and a child shows you they can do it independently 4 times then that means they are secure in that context and are ready to deepen their learning. I used to be guilty of making children, who were confident with a skill, repeat that skill for pages and pages because I believed it helped them retain it. This was not great for two reasons:

1. It was wasting their learning time – giving them a challenge or investigation where they applied their new skill in a different context would have been more efficient and better for their learning.

2. It meant a huge amount of time was spent marking pages and pages of correct answers – this didn't tell me anything more than just marking 4 correct answers. It also meant I was wasting lots of my own time as well as theirs.

The beauty of "4 and explore" is that you can mark all answers within the lesson, move on the children who need moving on and carry out targeted teaching with those who need more input on the skill.

Talking is a very useful tool for children.

Silence has its place in a classroom but so does talking. Managing and constructing meaningful opportunities for pupils to discuss, wonder, practice answers, work in groups and many more, allows for rapid learning. After all, if they can't say it, how can you expect them to write it? I find a busy, buzzing classroom a wonderful place to be – you can hear the learning and excitement about learning all around you. Again, you must set your expectations of talk within the classroom, model them, repeat them and practise, practise, practise.

The things I wish I knew about...

Personal Development

Listen to all feedback but don't take it personally.

There will be many people, on many occasions, who will give you feedback. At times it can seem like it is coming at you from all directions and you get into a position where you really don't know what to do. It can also feel as if you can't do anything right. Sometimes feedback can absolutely baffle you – "Your lesson was ok but I couldn't help but notice your shirt came untucked," was a particular favourite from my student year.

The worst thing about the amount of feedback you receive, especially early in your career, is that it can sometimes contradict what someone else said to you recently. This can be confusing and extremely demoralising. When this happens, it is important you discuss it with a mentor, coach or trusted colleague. Approach it in a professional way and state the facts and that you are confused. Sometimes there are too many people trying to help and support you and they either don't communicate, or just do not know each other.

People who give you feedback will also have different motivations and reasons for feedback – for example: An English Leader will have targets linked to English and therefore will give you targets and feedback linked to things that will raise attainment and progress in English. A Maths leader will have targets linked to Maths and will therefore give you targets linked to attainment and progress in Maths. A mentor will have your targets from previous observations and will link feedback to your development. A senior leader will have school priorities (not always overlapping with your development or subject specific targets) and will give you feedback linked to these. There are many more people with many different motivations and agendas who will enter your classroom and give you feedback. It can be overwhelming and can get very difficult at times.

It is important to remember that feedback is supposed to be given as part of the developmental process and should be well meant. You physically cannot act on everything you are told – it is impossible. You need to focus on the things that will have most impact on your daily practice and help you develop the quickest. Some feedback will be eye-opening and may help you revolutionise your teaching; other feedback will seem strange and have no impact on you as a professional. Either way, be positive – you can decide which parts of feedback are relevant to you and which parts you may choose to file away in your deepest darkest corner of your memory.

Building a good relationship with a mentor, coach, leader or colleague, who you can discuss feedback with will help you process and filter the many pointers you will receive.

Don't worry or over prepare for observations – do what you normally do.

I used to be obsessed with being "outstanding," and bought and read many books about becoming an "outstanding," teacher. I used to spend hours and hours preparing intricate "show lessons," for the benefit of my observer. Often these lessons did not go brilliantly because I was trying something different that my class didn't really understand.

I was glad when individual lesson grading was removed because it removed the focus on that 60 minutes of your practice. Observers should not be looking for a 60 minute "show lesson". They should be looking at how the lesson they observe fits into an ongoing sequence of learning that is making sure all children are **making progress over time**.

I am not advocating that you spend no time preparing and making sure you are organised for observed lessons (we want to show off our best selves) but I am advocating that you do not spend hours and hours making hundreds of resources and beautiful power points that we would not normally use.

My advice for observations are:

1. Look at any previous targets you had and make sure you show that you have acted

towards them – within your normal classroom routine.

2. Do not fall into the trap of speaking for extended periods of time (unless this is your school policy and normal practice) – the observer is there to observe learning, not watch you.

3. Be yourself – if you try and put on an act the children WILL give you away.

4. If everything is going wrong (which happens to all of us at times) do what you would normally do if there was no one there – don't just push on because you have planned it, if it has gone wrong then bring the children back together, discuss why it has gone wrong and go in whatever direction you need to make sure learning continues.

5. Be prepared – have everything ready that you need and make sure you know where it is. Check it!

6. If you have another adult in your team, make sure they know what they are doing and who they are doing it with.

7. Be confident – you are doing an excellent job and we are all learning all of the time. We will never ever be the finished article so this is just one step on your journey.

8. DO WHAT YOU NORMALLY DO.

9. After, take time to reflect and look at the positive things that happened. It is far too easy to focus solely on the negatives.

10. If it didn't go as well as you had hoped then remember the story I am going to tell you now...

I was three weeks into my first year of teaching and I was being observed by a member of the Senior Leadership Team for the first time. It was my time to shine! I planned a 'fantastic' maths lesson where pupils had to match questions to the corresponding answers. In my wisdom, I also decided to take this lesson outside. I got the children ready and my observer went to get her thick coat – it was a chilly, breezy Yorkshire day. We walked outside and my teaching assistant spread the questions and answers out around the tarmac area, as I explained what I wanted the children to do. Then, a scream! A girl in my class had been stung on the neck by a wasp. Little did we know, she was allergic and began to have a reaction. My teaching assistant and I quickly decided that she would take the child in for immediate attention and I would continue the lesson. As I turned back to the class, a particularly strong gust of wind blew and I watched in horror as my resources were spread across the surrounding fields. My observer observed, and I observed her scribbling notes on a clipboard. The children were in uproar – some tried to help as if in the final chamber of Crystal Maze; others sat and tried to look sensible; some decided it was a perfect opportunity to wrestle and fight! I did not know what to do. My observer did... she turned and walked away, leaving me to dread my feedback.

Needless to say, it wasn't the best feedback I have ever had and I know for a fact that the Senior Leaders questioned why I was there, but here I am many years later, much improved as a teacher and armed with the knowledge to never take paper outside on a windy day. And who knew that wasps were still around on a wintery September day!

So, no matter what happens in your observations, things could always be worse!

Use social media for the power of good.

I have found social media is a wonderful resource for teachers. I have borrowed many ideas for lessons, wider leadership and general resources. There are many fantastic educators on social media and I suggest all teachers create a twitter account and follow some of this list:

@teachertoolkit / @RossMcgill – the most followed teacher and publisher of great blogs about education.

@chrisdysonHT – Head teacher and National Leader of Education, champion of wellbeing and positivity.

@thatboycanteach – a primary Deputy Head and prolific, research/evidence based blogger.

@cazzash – a primary Deputy Head and champion for gender equality and great child-led learning.

@MrBoothY6 – a leading tweeter about reading in schools and how to use technology to support progress and learning.

@smithsmm – Primary Head teacher and champion for quality children's literature.

And of course... me - @sirmobbsalot

There are many, many more but these will be a good introduction to 'Edu twitter'.

My word of warning for social media – use it for the power of good. There are many people who paint a picture of a perfect classroom, school life, behaviour etc. Remember, not many people post their negatives so don't let it get you down.

Also, there are some on social media who seem to want to draw others into arguments. Education is a field where there are many opposing views and many evidence based studies to support different approaches. Decide on your beliefs and make them great but don't force them on others or feel you must justify/fight your own corner.

Think before you post online.

You will have training on this but really listen. There will be days you feel the need to rant or cry or explode – this may be because of your children or a colleague. SOCIAL MEDIA IS NOT AND NEVER WILL BE THE PLACE TO DO THIS! Don't even go there, it is seriously not worth it.

Create strong networks.

Teaching is a fantastic profession but it can be hard and isolating. Building a wide network that you can call upon is vital for several reasons:

1. **Wellbeing** – having people to talk to is essential. You will face regular challenges as a teacher, it happens to everyone. Trying to face these alone is a natural desire as we all want to appear strong and in control but it is fine to ask for support, help, guidance (or just have a good rant to someone).

2. **Resources** – time is such a valuable commodity and there never seems to be enough of it during the teaching year. Borrowing, sharing, copying resources from your network is an amazing time saver. Often, a resource already exists so being able to ask a network, rather than create it from scratch, saves valuable time. (Remember to give as well as take).

3. **Continued Professional Development** – building a wider network opens many doors in terms of your own development. Whether it be getting to know experienced colleagues who can share their wisdom; senior leaders who can act as career mentors; or just finding out about high-quality events – a network allows you access all of this and more.

4. **Jobs/Promotions** – you never know when you will want to move on from your current position and knowing a wide range of people makes this transition easier. Every person you meet could be a potential future employer.

For example, when I moved on from my first school I found out about the job opening from a trusted mentor. My new head teacher was a local authority moderator I had met several years before. I got the job on merit but knowing people helped get the wheels rolling.

Teaching is full of acronyms – if you don't know then ask.

NQT, EAL, PP, SEN, SEND, NEETs and many, many more. People in the profession can easily forget that those who are new do not know the definitions behind the hundreds of acronyms that become part of the daily language of schools. I still come across acronyms that I don't know! Worst of all, different schools/authorities/Academy trusts have different terminology to describe the same thing and therefore different acronyms.

Don't feel silly about asking what it means. Just go for it… it isn't your fault you don't know.

Your books are your emissaries.

There will be many judgements made about you as a teacher from viewing your books because it is one of the measures of 'progress over time'. Make sure you are clear about what you want in them and how your expectations effect this. How do you want these books to reflect you as a teacher when you are not there? If you accept poor presentation and low standards – what message is this sending about you as a teacher?

It is important for the children to experience high expectations and to develop pride in their work. It is just as important for you as the teacher to make sure that you are proud of every piece of work and every page. Too many times do I see teachers panicking before a book scrutiny and being very selective about the books they want to be seen. I encourage you to be the teacher who is proud of every book and confident that no matter which are picked they will reflect you in a positive light.

Take time to visit all year groups.

If you are in primary education, it can be too easy to get focused on your own year group and never see anything else. It is essential that you know where your children have come from and where they are going. Also, you never know which year group you might get the following year. I suggest you try and spend some time in each year group and get to know the curriculum expectations.

Read lots of children's fiction.

There is a wealth of children's fiction available and this should become your bread and butter. A major part of our role is to engage and excite children about reading – at times they will actively avoid it! The more you know about it and the more passionate you are about it the more your children will engage. It is hard to make recommendations when you don't know the subject matter. Keep an eye on the best seller lists on amazon and use your network to keep up to date on current excellent books.

The more you write, the better at teaching writing you become.

I found teaching writing very difficult until I became a writer myself. It is hard to understand the challenges of filling a blank page unless you have tried it yourself. Start a blog, keep a journal, write an e-book, write a novel – whatever it is it will really help. I have also found that my classes have been more motivated to write knowing that I am actively writing. They begged me to read them some of my fiction writing, which I gladly did. I had never seen them so quiet and engaged in a story (even if it was to find my mistakes and give me feedback).

Understanding and using data is useful.

During my training, I was asked to write a letter to myself about the type of teacher I wanted to be. This was mailed to me after I completed my first year in the classroom. In this letter, I promised myself I would never see children as statistics. With data pressure for progress and attainment this has been a hard promise to keep but I pride myself of seeing the whole child as a person.

Having said that, knowing about data and how to use it certainly helps you as a teacher. Firstly, it helps you identify trends and target children and focus your teaching accordingly. Secondly, it is a valuable skill that not everyone can do – this makes you valuable and can support your move into leadership roles (if this is your aim).

Don't be afraid to make mistakes and admit to them.

Learning to teach and teaching as a profession is hard. Nobody is perfect and nobody gets through a week in the classroom without making numerous mistakes.

I make mistakes all the time, mainly due to my atrocious, over-worked, memory. If you are honest and admit to mistakes and apologise where necessary then everything is usually fine. I have forgotten about appointments, introduced youth workers as nurses, mixed up times and dates and many more diary based mistakes. I have got maths problems wrong during my explanations. I have (on a handful of occasions) spelt words wrong. I'm still here and still going strong.

Once, during an OFSTED inspection, I forgot to put a question mark on a question I had hastily written on the board... my stomach lurched as I heard the inspector say to a child, "What has your teacher forgotten here? Does he do that often?" Then I smiled as my pupil replied, "No, but he does tell us that mistakes are part of learning and nothing to be sad about...innit."

So, remember – we are all learning every day. Mistakes happen. Admit to them and learn from them.

"Your aim is to show progress over time." – What does this mean?

This phrase confused and befuddled me for the first few years of my teaching career. I knew my children were learning and improving in many areas but I did not know how to "evidence" this.

Some schools do termly, or half termly tests to measure progress but I believe this is a flawed measure as it only assesses how that child did in that brief period on that day. Having said that, the results can be useful if used correctly e.g. to create target interventions, guide teaching and learning in specific directions to fill gaps in knowledge, show improvements in test conditions.

So, to show "progress over time," without relying in tests has been a tricky one. At a the most basic level it is: *In September they could not do this. Now they can.*

There are several ways to evidence progress:

1. *Assess children's weaknesses and teach specific skills to address them.*

E.g. If there is a group of children in maths who struggle to use column addition, teach that group strategies for column addition, let them rehearse/practise and give them feedback. Keep going until they get it. The progress will be evident in books, as will your targeted teaching.

2. *Make sure your teaching sequences (over time) include skill progression.*

E.g. In September, you probably won't be teaching use of semi-colons because unless commas and conjunctions are used accurately, it is difficult to use a semi-colon. Once the children can use commas and conjunctions then you would "progress" the skills you teach to include semi-colons. If someone looked at your books, they would see evidence of progress over time like this:

Sept – writing included low level conjunctions and some misused commas.

Nov – writing included a range of conjunctions and mostly accurate commas.

Jan – writing included a full range of conjunctions and accurate commas; teaching of semi-colons and colons seen.

March – writing included full range of conjunctions and commas, semi-colons and colons used accurately.

3. *Don't let children keep repeating the same mistakes.*

Whether this be a spelling, a misconception, apostrophes in plurals, letter formation errors, whatever it is you need to ensure it is not an ongoing problem. Once you spot it, make sure you give the child feedback and get them to practise and check their own work for the mistake. These mistakes disappearing is a great indicator of progress over time.

Warning: avoid constantly giving written marking about the same thing because this shows that you are not having an impact on that area. I would suggest that either you write it once and then have evidence of the work you got the child to do to address the error; or (better still) don't write anything and give the child verbal feedback and some tasks to do to improve their errors.

4. Presentation

Presentation can be a double victory to evidence progress over time.

i – If you set high expectations for presentation (rulers used, handwriting matches school policy, letters on lines, numbers in boxes, dates spelt correctly, no doodling/scribbling etc) then presentation naturally improves over time. It is such an easy way to show progress to flick from a September page to a Later Date page and look at the improvements.

ii. Impressions are a massive part of looking at books. People will pretend they are not but repeatedly I have seen people make immediate judgements due to presentation – it's human nature. If a book is dog-eared, doodled on, lots of scribbling, rulers not used, poor handwriting, then it immediately means the person looking at it perceives it as being low quality. If a book is beautifully presented then the person perceives quality and care.

I didn't truly realise the importance of presentation until I became a leader with responsibility for work scrutiny (book looks, book dips, monitoring, quality control, whatever it may be called in different establishments). I encourage you to set your standards in September (higher than you think possible) and stick to them.

Embrace training opportunities – it's always good to learn new things.

When you are extremely busy (and you will be), training sessions can seem like a waste of time. You might feel that the hour or two you have to spend in a session could have been utilised better elsewhere. In some cases you are right, however, the more you embrace training the faster things will start to make sense.

There are some sessions you might have wanted to skip that change your entire outlook on teaching and you go back to the classroom buzzing about all the new things you learnt. There are others that will not be quite as good but I encourage you to try and take at least one thing from every session because, over time, they will compound to become hundreds of things. For example, if you had a training session every week of the year and you took one thing from each session then you have 52 new things that you know or can use. If you did this for 5 years, you would have 260 things. (I know we don't teach 52 weeks of the year – thank goodness – but you can still learn new things when out of the school calendar). This does not include the sessions where you will take 2, 3, 5, 10, 20 things.

Remember you are on a journey to learn to be an excellent teacher, all training is part of that journey and the more you embrace it, the more effective it will be.

Surround yourself with mentors.

Mentors come in all shapes and sizes, in both official and unofficial capacities. You will have an assigned mentor who is your day to day support system. You might have a university or college coach/mentor. You may be provided with a coach/mentor from your training provider. Make the most of these relationships.

Further to this, build relationships with a wider network of mentors: colleagues, consultants, head teachers, deputy head teachers, on social media, at conferences... wherever. Make the most of the knowledge and skills that the people around you possess. You never know when you might need a favour or some sage advice.

Set yourself goals.

You will be given targets linked to your performance and generally one or two linked to data outcomes for your children. This is not what I am talking about in this section.

I encourage you to set yourself personal career goals: short term, medium term, long term and visionary. This allows you to stay focussed on YOU alongside your classes and school.

Examples of these:

Short term (Inside a half term: check in every week or two) –

- Whilst training, get all assignments in a week early and have a break during half term.
- Meet all targets set by mentor.
- Attend a training session about assessment.

Medium Term (Inside a year: check in every couple of months) –

- Complete student year with good or better assessment grades.

or

- Complete NQT year and secure a job.

or

- Have a TLR for leading a subject.

Long Term (1-5 years: check in every 6 months) –

- Be a member of Senior Leadership within 5 years.

Or

- Have taught in more than one key stage.

Or

- Start a successful education blog and write a book.

Visionary (More than 5 years: check in every year) –

- Be Head teacher of a nationally recognised 'Outstanding' School.

Or

- Run a social enterprise project addressing an area of social deprivation.

Or

- Be an excellent teacher and have a successful work life balance.

Obviously, your targets will be personal to you but be as ambitious as you want. Have things to aim for and this will keep you focussed over an extended period of time. Pick targets that **you** believe in, not what you think others would want you to do. Don't be embarrassed by them... they are yours.

Stay on top of any paperwork / assignments you have.

I always promised myself that I would do this and I rarely did. On the occasions where I did manage myself and finish work early, I had a much better outlook on teaching. It meant I could have a few days off in half term holidays rather than be doing assignments when I was shattered from a full half term of teaching. It is difficult but doing a little bit over a long time is better than saving it all up for the holiday when you NEED to relax and re-charge.

Keep track of any evidence of your impact.

It is an excellent idea to keep track of any actions you take that make a difference in your classroom, the wider school or education in general. It makes performance management much easier and applying for jobs when the time comes.

I keep a week by week diary on my computer where I fill in my actions and intended impact. I then keep track of these and attach any data, feedback or improvements that occur because of my actions. It is also a great record to look back at because there are many things you do and don't really think about that make massive improvements for your children, colleagues, school and beyond. Be proud of yourself!

The things I wish I knew about...

Relationships

You will be given many random things by children.

This will be an almost daily occurrence: walking down the corridors, in the classroom, in the dinner hall, before school, after school. Children will thrust drawings, letters, objects and much more into your hands and exclaim, "I made this for you," and sometimes get your name wrong. It can sometimes be when you are busy or on the way somewhere but I encourage you to take the time to thank the child; ask them about it; tell them that it means a lot to you. It may seem insignificant or an inconvenience to you but they have spent time on it and chosen you to pass it on to. Make the most of these opportunities to build relationships. What you do with it afterwards is up to you: I have a wall behind my desk where gifts/letters go.

You will be the best teacher in the world... until they talk to another teacher.

"Sir, you're my favourite teacher." "Miss, you're my joint favourite teacher with __ (insert name of another teacher in ear shot____)," It happens all the time but that doesn't mean you can't enjoy it, just don't be disappointed when their love moves on as quickly as it arrived.

Have lunch with the children – they love it.

I always find having lunch with children an amazing experience. You can gain so much from the informal conversations that occur and use this to strengthen your relationships with your class and beyond. Also, the children absolutely love it and will clamour for your attention and to sit next to you. I have seen "lunch with a teacher," used as a reward for children making the right choices. Try and do this once a week and see the impact it has in your classroom.

Trust and respect is a currency built up through hundreds of interactions and repeated messages.

You can read as many "behaviour management" books as you want and attend as many training sessions that you can, but the crux of effective "behaviour management" (other than consistency) is trust and respect. If the children trust and respect you then they are more willing to follow your lead, do as you ask and go above and beyond.

Not all children will trust and respect you solely because you are a teacher, this honour must be earned. It is built up through every conversation, every message you send, body language, how you deal with situations and the consistency of just showing up and being there.

I always find the first half term the hardest in terms of behaviour because you are getting to know the children and they are getting to know you. The trust and respect has not yet been built and they naturally want to push you to see your boundaries and expectations.

So, get to know your children as well as you can, be consistent and keep turning up day after day. They will soon realise that you genuinely care about them and in some cases, will become fiercely protective of you. Some days it feels hard but it comes in time and will be worth it.

Children know when you genuinely care about them.

Children are very astute – they can soon tell how you really feel about them. I make sure I constantly message to them that I care about them and their futures. I take every opportunity to tell them this individually and as a group. They may not believe you at first but once you tell them for the tenth, fiftieth, hundredth time then it starts to sink in. When they believe this then they start to genuinely care about you to and everything becomes a lot smoother and easier.

Build good relationships with parents – get outside and meet them.

Parents are a hugely important part of the school system but are a massively underutilised resource. Getting them onside and involved helps you in all areas of teaching. It is far better to have relationships with parents than not – especially if you may have to ring them regularly to report instances of poor behaviour.

At times it may feel like you are at odds with some parents but always remember that they just want the best for their child (even if they may not always show it). If you have a good relationship these challenging situations can be much easier than if you are meeting for the first time.

I always try and meet the parents as often as I can by going out after school, chatting, telling them about brilliant things their children have done and talking about upcoming events. I think it is important to be a presence physically as well as verbally – it is too easy to be just a name on a piece of paper or spoken about at the dinner table. Get to know them and use the relationships to your advantage.

Communicate constantly – if there is an issue address it at the time; parents don't like surprises.

Communication is essential – especially to parents.

1. Incidents such as falling out, fighting, getting hurt, bumps, bangs, scrapes etc

What may seem like a small or innocuous incident to you can all too quickly spiral out of control and become a massive issue for parents. An incident explained by their child can be one sided and greatly exaggerated. It is far better to get out ahead of a problem and speak to them face to face or make a phone call to explain what happened.

2. Ongoing issues with a child

Speaking to parents as soon as a child shows signs of repeated poor behaviour is important. Sometimes it feels like you are moaning, however, if you don't tell them then when it truly comes to a point of further action then it can be a surprise and met with resistance. It is far too late to tell them at parents evening or in a report.

3. Great stuff

Communication should not only be for negative things. It brings you down and the parents who only ever receive the, "I need to tell you about _____ behaviour again," call.

Make positive phone calls, have positive meetings – let them know all the great stuff that is happening in your classroom and school.

Remember – they are trusting you with the most precious thing in their world, keep them informed and try your best not to surprise them.

Close windows, lock doors, turn lights off.

I would suggest you have an 'end of day' routine where you take ownership of your own classroom. Close all your windows, lock any doors that need locking and turn off anything that needs turning off. If you don't then someone else has to. Saving them small amounts of time will add up over time and will be much appreciated.

Get to know the caretaker/site manager.

Things break in schools and the caretaker always has an extensive list to complete. Having a good relationship with them will magically make your 'urgent' jobs be seen to quicker. You never know when you might need to call on them for a favour. It works two ways as well, if you see them doing a job you could help with then do it: I have carried cupboards, emptied classrooms into skips, constructed furniture and much more. In return, my jobs tend to get done straight away, the caretaker goes above and beyond in their own time to help and best of all... one brought me a cream cake (she used to be a baker; it was INCREDIBLE)!

Get to know kitchen staff.

It is very easy to never speak to anyone who works in the kitchen as they keep different hours to you and tend to be hidden away behind roller shutters or closed doors. I encourage you to make the effort to get to know the whole team. Find out the health and safety rules before you just barge in (some kitchens ask staff not to enter) but have conversations, take dirty plates back, say thank you. It is a valuable relationship to have. I previously mentioned my terrible memory; the kitchen team have rescued me on a few occasions. When I forget my lunch and wallet – the kitchen has trusted me enough to provide my lunch and let me pay later. When I forget to give them the required notice about a trip – they still provide packed lunches without too much grumbling. One kitchen manager used to bring me a bacon sandwich some mornings because "You look tired."

Get to know office staff.

The office staff can make your life so much easier and they are a huge part of any school team. They always know everything that is happening in school, control the diary, book rooms for you when needed, make phone calls, emails, book external/internal events, are the first line against angry parents, send letters, give first aid, have all the forms you could ever need and so much more. If you have a good relationship with them then they will be more willing to help you which in turn will save you vast amounts of time. I encourage you to make the effort to get to know all the office staff and have regular conversations with them, don't just turn up when you need a job doing.

Get to know IT maintenance staff.

Computers and technology are such a useful part of schools and can add huge value to learning. But, in my experience, it often fails at the vital moment. Something goes wrong and even the most IT savvy teachers struggle to fix it. This is where a good relationship with the 'IT guys' is essential. They are busy and sometimes will only visit schools once or twice a week. Get to know them, have conversations, build that relationship – it will save you at some point!

Get to know cleaning staff.

This can be difficult as you may only cross paths fleetingly before or after school finishes. Make sure you say hello and get to know a bit about them. Ask them how they are doing and tell them bits about yourself. They do an incredible job and deserve thanking for it. Once, after a papier-mache lesson, one of my wonderful children had decided to 'wash' their mixture down the classroom sink. Little did I know that the mixture hardens in the pipes and on the metal sink and dries like concrete. My cleaner worked for well over an hour to fix the situation and didn't complain at all. I only found out weeks later from a member of the office staff (as previously stated – they know everything). Next time I saw her I apologised and thanked her.

The things I wish I knew about...

Teaching Practice

"There is no magic book of lesson plans to refer to" (@MrTRoach)

Thanks to @MrTRoach for this suggestion. It is very true! When you enter most professions there are manuals, guides, systems and central resources to access. This is not the case in teaching and it very much took me by surprise. We have the national curriculum and then schools can essentially teach this however they want. As a teacher you are given a fantastic opportunity to be creative, innovative and independent with how you deliver lessons. This can be daunting though as it is not always obvious how to best teach a concept, skill, or piece of knowledge. It would sometimes be nice to have a magic book of lesson plans to refer to.

(This is where being a member of a community/network is useful because you can ask people who have done it before and share their experience and resources).

There are websites and companies who do provide resources and plans (some free and some charged). The two I have had greatest success with are:

1. https://www.tes.com/teaching-resources (a free to join website where teachers can share resources and plans. They have recently added the option for teachers to charge others for some resources. The overall quality of resources is good but I suggest you always

thoroughly check, and change them to suit your class, before using).

2. https://www.twinkl.co.uk/ (A subscription website that is growing rapidly. Resources and plans are provided for pretty much all topics and subjects. A very useful time saving site with very good quality resources created by teachers for teachers.)

You don't necessarily need to use resources and plans from others because sometimes you will need something more specific to your class or individual child. I would suggest you do use them sometimes though because the best advice I had early in my career was, "Why reinvent the wheel?". If there is something out there that you can access that is good, then why spend hours making your own for the same outcome. Save yourself some time and invest it somewhere else.

Make opportunities to visit as many different schools as possible.

Teachers can become ultra-focussed on their own classroom and class. Once you find a way of doing things that suits you then that can be it (whether it is 100% effective or not). I have got so much out of visiting different schools, seeing how they structure their day, how they teach different subjects, how they run break and lunchtimes, different displays and how different values and ethos effect the wider school. If you cherry pick the ideas you like and implement them at your school, then you will constantly improve as a teacher and leader. Don't get trapped in the four walls of your classroom – look outward and steal all the great ideas that are out there and provide opportunities for other people to share yours.

Observe as many other teachers as you can.

Similarly, the more you can get out of your classroom and observe other teachers the better. You will notice the amazingly subtle nuances that experienced teachers demonstrate. You will see opportunities to assess taken (and missed). You will see excellent behaviour management and not so great behaviour management. The more you see the more you will learn. I think joint observations are one of the best learning tools for a new teacher – it allows you to see the lesson through an experienced colleague's eyes and analyse it together. I encourage you to request the opportunity to spend time in as many different classrooms with as many different teachers as possible. I did this during a teaching placement at an 'outstanding' school and the science lesson I saw completely transformed my practice. This would not have happened if I was having a cup of coffee in the staffroom. Be proactive, make and take the opportunities to see great practitioners wherever possible.

Borrow good-ideas as often as you can.

You do not have to deliver completely unique and original lessons and ideas all the time. Yes, it is a great part of the job to invent lessons and resources and tailor them to your pupils but great teachers also know a great idea when they see one. Borrow, 'magpie', steal the best ideas you see and use them in your own practice. Treat your class to a constant stream of amazing lessons and sequences to engage and excite them in learning. Save yourself time by not having to think of them yourself all the time.

Embed new techniques into normal practice – things take more attempts than one or two.

I always come back from training courses or conferences buzzing with new ideas. I try them in the classroom and they work (or don't), then I try them again the next day and they work (or don't) but gradually the 'new' technique/activity falls by the wayside and is replaced by a 'newer' technique or I fall back into my 'old' way of doing things.

If you find a technique/activity that has good impact on engagement and progress in your classroom then use it regularly. Challenge yourself to use it a couple of times a week. Train your children to do it well and continue to use it. Grow your toolkit of teaching techniques and try not to forget the brilliant things you did in the wave of post-training-enthusiasm.

Teaching assistants are AMAZING.

I was a teaching assistant before becoming a teacher and I always preferred to be told exactly what was needed from me. Far too often I found teachers to be shy to ask me to do jobs for them and I ended up sitting and watching lessons.

If you are lucky enough to have another adult in your classroom, treasure them! They are dedicated, hardworking and a massive part of your support network. Get to know them, find out their passions, skills, interests and make the most of these in the classroom. I had an excellent illustrator once and he led most of our art lessons; another was fluent in French so delivered French lessons across the school. Don't miss these opportunities.

They are an unbelievably valuable resource but you need to use them right. If you find that your additional adult is 'sitting and watching' you talk then you need to direct them more effectively. Allocate them a group of children;

give them ownership of a target such as handwriting or spelling; ask them to listen to children read. During lesson time, additional adults should be advancing pupils' learning at all times. I hate to see teaching assistants wasted by laminating, cutting out, sticking, doing displays etc. Plan for them, direct them and reap the rewards of these dedicated and supportive people.

Read, read, read.

You are clearly already on top of this as you are reading this now. The more you read, the more you will develop your own pedagogy and beliefs about teaching. Whatever you believe and however you approach education, remember that others will have different opinions, beliefs and approaches.

Read blogs, books, documents, forums, social media threads – anything linked to the area of education you most need to improve/have most interest in. You will find yourself filling up with knowledge and as a result your teaching practice will improve. Implement the things you discover and embed them into your practice. You are not alone, you do not have to do/invent everything yourself... learn from those who have been before you and be brilliant.

A lesson should never take longer to plan and resource than it should to deliver.

If a lesson is 45-60 minutes long then it should not take 2 hours to plan and resource.

I used to spend hours making lengthy power points, colourful resources, laminating, cutting things out and creating all my other bells and whistles... for... every ... single... lesson. And then I wondered why I had no time for family, friends, gym, rugby or life in general. Planning lessons is a skill and certainly needs careful thought to be successful. It is something that does get easier and faster with experience but be sensible when you start – do not make extra work for yourself when you will already be the busiest you have ever been.

It is great to have these wow lessons every now and then because it completely hooks children into the topic/subject. In these instances, the time/benefit cost is worth it because it stretches far beyond the individual lesson. It is unsustainable to plan and deliver lessons like this two or three times a day.

An example from my student year in an observed lesson: I had created my usual power point, with cool transitions, sound effects and pictures, to structure the lesson and created 5 different sets of resources – one for each of my groups. I delivered the lesson and it went as planned – it was an ok lesson. It had taken me over two hours to prepare and resource. My observer asked me to show him my power point and talk him through each slide. Once I had finished he asked me to look at how many slides I had created. 42. He pointed out that I had spent less than 10 seconds on some of the slides and that many of them were not useful or relevant to the learning. He then modelled how to get the same information across in 5 slides or fewer. I was working hard but I was not working smart. I was making myself very busy for very little or no impact.

Don't fall into this trap. Most of the time the best lessons come with very little physical preparation. It is the clinical thinking of the teacher and the choice of low/no prep activities that lead to the most effective learning for the children. Working harder is not always better.

Be yourself.

You can create a teacher persona and practise this until it becomes second nature but I have found that being yourself is the best way to be. It is too hard to sustain an act for 6 hours a day. If you are funny then be funny. If you are quiet then be your quiet self. If you are consistent and ready the same in the same situations then you are all good.

Use your hobbies and interests to engage and excite your children. All my classes know about rugby union and the values that are part of the sport. I saw one class that were obsessed by Japanese anime because the teacher was passionate and had shared this with them. This extends to whole school as well – the best schools I have seen are an extension of the leadership. One school I visited had a football-mad head teacher, as a result PE was held in high esteem, there were regular training sessions for the school team and they won most tournaments they entered. Another amazing school I worked with had a head teacher who loved being outdoors and nature, as a result the entire wonderful curriculum of the school was based around entitlements for being outdoors, going on trips and experiencing nature – one of her mottos was: "There is no bad weather, just the wrong clothes." Those children were outside no matter what (I visited in a snow storm where the playground was sheet ice and the children were outside, slipping and falling constantly, learning about friction – or the lack of it).

If you are yourself and bring your passion about whatever you love then this will rub off on your children. You are not vanilla so don't act like it!

Be consistent.

I have mentioned this a few times because it will make or break you. You must develop the ability to apply your expectations exactly the same, for everyone, no matter the situation.

Whether you are busy, tired, stressed, poorly or not had coffee yet, you must be absolutely fair and consistent. Children are absolute champions for fairness and they will sniff out inconsistency immediately. They will be livid if you gave them a sanction 6 months ago but don't give their friend one for doing exactly the same thing today. They will absolutely let you know if it's not fair.

Imagine a referee in a top-class sporting event. Their job is to apply the rules of the game absolutely evenly to both teams. If a referee is inconsistent then the players lose control, the fans are in uproar and in the end the referee will lose their job. You are the referee in your classroom – it can be challenging but be consistent and fair at all times.

Decide on your system and implement it fairly to every child. Sometimes you might feel harsh giving your brilliant child who always makes the right choices a consequence if they do make a poor choice but you can't let them off because if you do the children who do not always make the right choices will see this and jump on it. You have to do it.

Get risk assessments and paperwork for trips planned well in advance.

These are part of every trip/event and can be one of the most time sapping jobs there is. I have been guilty of leaving them to the last minute and then stressing to get them in by the deadline. They are not fun but I suggest you do them as far in advance as possible. I recommend you contact wherever you are going and ask if they have a risk assessment and if they can send it to you – this will save you huge amounts of time. I also suggest once you have written one for a coach or minibus that you save it and use it for future trips – this will save you time as well. Get them done, get them checked, then don't worry about them.

Use shortcuts wherever possible.

This is something I wish someone had told me Day 1, week 1 of teacher training. There will always be too much work to get done in the time available to you. You could work every second you are awake and never get to the end of your to do list. This means you need to take a very proactive approach to your workload. When you add a task to your list you must ask yourself – what is the quickest way I can accomplish this with the least amount of time and effort. I'm not saying rush things or don't produce your best, I'm saying be ultimately efficient. If there is a shortcut, use it! Work smarter, not harder. Save every second you can and invest it in your own well-being. A less tired, less stressed version of you with slightly less preparation will be a much more effective presence in the classroom.

Re-use resources in many ways.

If you do decide to invest your time making a resource then be creative with it. Can it be used in more than one way? Can the model writing you spent ages creating be used for the writing lesson but also for reading, grammar, spelling and handwriting sessions? Why create 5 things if one thing can be used 5 times? Be efficient and clever with resources you make. Can you store them to use later? Be organised for computer generated resources – have a system where you save them by skill/topic/genre, whatever helps you quickly find them next time you need them. Create, use, adjust, re-use and so on.

Stay on top of marking.

I am very glad that there is a current move away from vast amounts of written marking. Having said this, many schools do still have policies that require written feedback. My advice is stay on top of this! Don't let it build up or it will become overwhelming and a major stressor. Use your time efficiently and try and get as much done during the day, with the children. Train them to mark elements of their own work, or each other's. Get your TA to mark their group. Have systems in place to ensure you are implementing the school marking policy and never fall behind. It is awful to have to catch up and once you are back marking it has lost any relevance or impact anyway.

Listen to children.

Children of all ages are incredible and you will learn a lot from listening to them. Follow their interests to engage them in their learning. Listen to when they tell you that so and so has done something to someone on the playground. Listen to them when they tell you about their home life. Just listen and give them the time they deserve. They have chosen to talk to you and that makes you special to them. If they want to talk to you at an inappropriate or inconvenient time just politely tell them that you will talk to them later and then make sure you do.

Don't label children due to prior attainment.

I am not a fan of ability labels. I really don't like terminology such as 'low ability, mid ability and high ability' because you are immediately judging a child on prior performance. There are many cognitive and behavioural reasons why children may not perform at the levels of their peers but this does not mean they cannot achieve the same outcomes if you provide the opportunities and support.

In my experience, children raise their standards to meet your expectations. If you set low expectations because they have previously performed at a low level then of course they will continue to perform at a low level as that is what you have set them up to do. No child wants to be in the 'low group' and once they perceive that that is the case then they feel different to their peers and many actively shift focus away from their 'ability' through challenging behaviour.

I taught a child who had been labelled "unteachable" because he had regular swearing outbursts, growled and was violent towards staff and other children. To be honest I was really worried about taking over his class. Once I got to know him and unpicked his behaviours by sitting with him and asking him, it turned out he hated feeling "different" to the other children because he was doing "baby" work. From that point forward, we ensured that the work he was doing was at an appropriate challenge but did not appear outwardly different. We paired him with a child who found the work less challenging and we raised his expectations of himself by raising our own. He no longer went out for 1:1 reading instead of being in for class sessions (he did this in an additional session). We reinforced constantly that he was no different and we expected nothing less from him than the others. He was a changed child because he realised he was the same as his peers and no longer felt like a baby – yes, he needed a huge amount of pre-teaching and additional support but it was worth the effort to see him develop into a hardworking, lovely member of the school community. (He still had the odd outburst of swearing every so often but he was no longer violent and always followed instructions even when angry).

Get resources ready in advance.

Be prepared. I always try and do any printing that I need (although I try and go paperless where I can) the day before I need it. There are several reasons for this:

1. The photocopier/printer is always busiest before school.
2. The photocopier/printer will break regularly.
3. The photocopier/printer will run out of paper or ink or both when you are in a rush
4. Having resources ready prevents you from planning and then replanning and changing your lesson that evening. You are committed to it and can leave work knowing you are ready.
5. If you are poorly then everything is prepared for whoever is covering you and you can concentrate on getting better rather than sending frantic emails at 7am.

Develop questioning techniques.

Questioning is an essential art to develop as a teacher and I say art deliberately. It is not as simple as asking a question, choosing the first hand up and then moving on. You ask questions for many reasons not just because that's what teachers have always done. I suggest you read a lot about questioning and the techniques involved – it is essential and will save you massive amounts of time because if you know exactly where every child is in terms of understanding then you don't waste time teaching them stuff they already know/understand. Join my mailing list and keep an eye out for "Things I wish I had known about Active Assessment."

Use what you find out from questioning.

When you have asked your question, and gained information from the children's answers then use it. If you suddenly realise that none of them understand what you are teaching then stop and go back a step to ensure they can come on the journey with you. Also, if you realise they have all understood quicker than you thought then move on to the next step. You don't have to do an activity based on something they already know how to do just because you have planned it. Don't waste time, use the information you expertly gained from your precise questioning.

Make sure your marking is responded to – it must show impact.

If you have to do written marking, make sure you give children something that they must respond to. It may be answering an extension question or editing their writing or rephrasing something (see Bloom's Taxonomy question stems for brilliant marking questions). Make sure you give them time to respond because you have spent ages doing it so it needs to have an impact. Writing "good work" in 30 books is an incredible waste of time. Say it to the child, it means more and saves you an hour. If you have to do written marking make sure it has an impact on learning.

The things I wish I knew about...

The World of Education

Know that every single person has an opinion about teaching/teachers – not all positive.

Education is a polarising profession. Everyone involved in it has staunch beliefs about the best way to do it and some are vocal in letting others know about it. People are undoubtedly influenced by their own experience of education, their training, their mentors, their colleagues and their wider reading. This is understandable but the debates that occur (particularly on platforms like twitter) can verge on abusive and can overstep the mark. I suggest you stay away from these arguments and concentrate on your own pedagogy and practice. Do not get drawn in and do not let anyone at any time dampen your enthusiasm for teaching. You have chosen to come into the profession for what will be very deep and personal reasons, stick to these and leave others to it.

Recognise that not all teachers are positive.

I pride myself on positivity. I trained with other very positive people. I have always been surrounded by positivity in my sports teams. I was very surprised by the jaded, worn out negativity that seemed rife in certain education settings. It almost seems as if some people take pride in draining the enthusiasm and positivity from those who are fresh to the profession. Be strong against this. Be the positive beacon who radiates throughout the school, take others with you and do not join 'the dark side'. Don't fall into education negativity – blaze your own trail.

Some leadership teams and schools won't suit you – don't be afraid to move on (@AnnaLambertini)

Thanks to @AnnaLambertini for this very true suggestion. I have found that schools are massively different places to work and a lot of that depends on the leadership culture. Too many teachers are leaving the profession because they find themselves in a culture that does not suit them but then they assume that all places in education are like that. It is not the case – there are wonderful places out there to work. Amazing cultures developed by exceptional leaders. Please don't feel trapped in a situation that makes you miserable, please do not walk away from teaching because of a poor school culture. Do your research, find a school with a great culture with a leader who inspires you. Remember why you became a teacher and move away from any situation that you are not happy in. You can do it.

Every teacher has lessons that go wrong.

Sometimes you will have a lesson that just does not work. It can come out of nowhere and you can try to rescue it but it just falls flat. What you planned might be too hard, the activity might be too confusing, a child might sabotage it deliberately or by accident, the wind might be blowing too hard, it might snow or worst of all a wasp or bee might enter the room. It happens to all of us so do not worry about it. Reflect on what happened. Talk it through with a colleague or mentor. Work out why it didn't work and let it go. Don't beat yourself up about it.

Ignore anyone who says teachers finish at 3 and have loads of holiday.

You earn every single second of your holiday. If anyone utters the above then I suggest you direct them to one of my favourite poems by Taylor Mali – What Teachers Make

https://www.ted.com/talks/taylor_mali_what_t eachers_make

There is a culture of "Work yourself to death or you're not trying hard enough." (@Matt23Leeds)

Thank you to @Matt23Leeds for this comment. I agree that there is certainly a common feeling within education that you need to be working so hard it feels as though you are at breaking point most of the time. Instances of mental illness are on the rise and many teachers must take lengthy periods of absence due to stress related problems. Teaching is not the only profession where this is the case but it does seem that teachers almost wear the workload as a badge of honour. I see statements on social media proudly announcing, "Marking until midnight #teaching.",

"Just leaving school with my 60 books,"

"Another weekend working."

And I have heard colleagues announce very similar things in numerous staff rooms. I believe that this is part of the ingrained problem in teaching.

The culture when you come into the profession is that you have to work until you drop, it is the job, it is the expectation. Indeed, when I told my mentor during first year that I was really struggling the response I got was "That's teaching." As a naïve student, I accepted this response and just worked harder until I got through to summer holidays, nearly having a breakdown on a couple of occasions. Now, I absolutely disagree! The job does require hard work and dedication (so do many others) but teaching as a profession brings much of the workload problems on itself due to the culture. We need a brave few to stand up against this culture and shift it towards wellbeing of our wonderful teaching force. It is beginning but I urge you to join the fight. Work smarter not harder. Don't make statements about ridiculous working hours because they make others feel like they should be doing the same. Question whether the task you are doing is worth the time and if it is work out how to do it in the most efficient manner. Have a wonderful, full life outside of teaching because what's the point in trying to create a brilliant future for your pupils if you are not enjoying the one you created for yourself?

The things I wish
I knew about...

Thank you very much for taking the time to read this book. I honestly hope you have read something that helps you in your career as a teacher. I believe you have made an excellent choice in becoming a teacher and joining the profession because it is the most fulfilling experience ever. You will face some tough times and challenges, it is going to happen. When you are finding it hard, like we all did and at times still do, please reach out to someone. If you want to reach out to me then I would be more than happy to talk things through with you – contact me on twitter @sirmobbsalot or Facebook https://fb.me/sirmobbsalot . I will respond to all messages as quickly as I can. If you do not need to reach out but you want to talk about anything you've read then feel free to contact me as well.

Please do not give up. Stick with it and become an amazing teacher! You will be the person who changes someone's life and there is no greater gift you can give.

Best of Luck.

Tim Mobbs

Twitter: @sirmobbsalot

Facebook:
https://www.facebook.com/sirmobbsalot/

Blog:
https://bebetterteachingblog.wordpress.com/
where you can join my mailing list to hear
regular hints and tips and about my new
publications.

Printed in Great Britain
by Amazon

37148007R00088